BY ROBERT KELLY

Armed Descent (1961)
Her Body Against Time (1963)
Round Dances (1964)
Enstasy (1964)
Lunes (1964)
Lectiones (1965)
Words In Service (1965)
Weeks (1966)
The Scorpions (1967)
Song XXIV (1967)
Devotions (1967)
Twenty Poems (1967)
Axon Dendron Tree (1967)
Crooked Bridge Love Society (1967)
A Joining (1967)
Alpha (1968)
Finding the Measure (1968)
Sonnets (1968)
Statement (1968)
Songs I-XXX (1968)
The Common Shore (1969)
A California Journal (1969)
Kali Yuga (1970)
Cities (1971)
In Time (1971)
Flesh Dream Book (1971)
Ralegh (1972)
The Pastorals (1972)
Reading Her Notes (1972)
The Tears of Edmund Burke (1973)
The Mill of Particulars (1973)
A Line of Sight (1974)
The Loom (1975)
Sixteen Odes (1976)
The Lady Of (1977)
The Convections (1978)
Wheres (1978)
The Book of Persephone (1978)
The Cruise of the Pnyx (1979)
Kill the Messenger Who Brings Bad News (1979)
Sentence (1980)
Spiritual Exercises (1981)
The Alchemist to Mercury (1981)
Mulberry Women (1982)
Under Words (1983)

Editor

A Controversy of Poets (1965)

ROBERT KELLY

UNDER WORDS

BLACK SPARROW PRESS
SANTA BARBARA — 1983

ACKNOWLEDGEMENT

These poems were composed between June 1980 and June 1982. Some of them have appeared in magazines: *Sulfur* (Clayton Eshleman), *Epoch* (Cecil Giscombe and Nancy Couto), *Eat it alive* (Normandi Ellis), *Continental Drift* (Tandy Sturgeon), but most appear here for the first time, following my sense of making a book less a gathering of already uttered texts, and more a new word.

LIBRARY OF CONGRESS CATALOGING IN PUBLICATION DATA

Kelly, Robert, 1935-
    Under words.

    I. Title.
PS3521.E4322U5   1983   811'.54   83-12325
ISBN 0-87685-595-8
ISBN 0-87685-594-X (pbk.)

A SELF-SECRET TEXT IN WHICH IS SHOWN A TRUE DEPARTURE
FROM THE UNDERWORLD, THE HUMID PATH REVERSED, THE
DRINK UNDRUNK AND THE CUP STILL FULL, A WINDOW
FULL OF STORIES AND MOHAMMED FALLING, HIS
GREEN ROBE A FLAME OF CONTRADICTORY
FIRE POINTING UP BUT GOING DOWN,
AND THE RED WOMAN FINALLY
EMBRACES HER PROPER MATE.
LYNCH PIN OF CREATION.
SINGLETREE OF YOKED
STARS, THE HIDDEN
WHOLE NUMBER
BETWEEN ONE
AND TWO
REVEALED
AT LAST

Table of Contents

UNDER WORDS

AUGURIES

for Kimberly Lyons

whipped only against the day

      after rain
      an animal

if we could link
the facts of our condition to

the animal it is to be in the world
grace
to be in the world alone

to be by tree
conceptualize your body
bent to your own occasions
moving between me and the freshening light

★   ★   ★

Pleiades overhead   sisters

      I want
     more than

I want my hair ruffled by your hand
your fingertips pressing my eyebrows and cheekbones

we are braille to each other also

boy who collected maps the names
reaching for what he could of a real person

names are the tits of things

punk dictionaries
always selling out the language we invent

* * *

you and I we invent
diversely
invent language
always fresh
the run of it

the milk

(later bland book bread dictionary cheese)

to force
the quiet rain

it is elegant to spurn
even our own accumulations

* * *

double reaching motives reach the moon

stepping onto the porch my retracted foot
upset the cat's water soaked
the heel of my sock the wet

sensation is the moment's life

                    your hands
                  on my face
whatever is given or taken hereafter *that* is given

The skin does not forget

                        *   *   *

bones are true

so old pictures show the skull
                            philosopher hand
                  resting on some skull

his own skull it will be, rememberer
                        of all that is actual

that let feeling live

it has something to do with the moon
the confusions
are native, it does not do
to solve them fast
where streets run towards us from the west

what do I want of you

space by intricate monad freed.

ANALYTIC HYMN

It rains even in California.
On such a night all cars look old but clean,
windshields sloshed clear.
I see your trim middle snug in satin,
white satin even, under
the marquee of Nick's Club.
You wait, faintly wiggling. The parker
        catches my keys and who am I.

Who am I. I am someone
who wants this situation, and that other one
when, your mouth soft and wise with gin,
you kiss me all the way down the freeway
while I release your body from its seeming.
I come inside you like an old movie.

My boyhood was a raft of poems
but the marsh was real, a light
I later claimed as William Mount's light,
smooth-faced miscegeny of flesh and water

and where Whitman saw the actual bird
and lifted it, a general of the Vast Imaged Nation,
I saw only angels. And from their turbulence
in water at the sedge roots I took
for my garment the burlap web of the particular,

ever after trying to find, and finding, that angel light
in this and that.

          My Paumanok
was an infinite book, but intricate and mine,
blurred adventures of all the old heroes
to become I simply am.
                Wherever I may have come from
it is enough now that down in the bay
a yacht leans forward in high wind,
spinnaker cheeked out, white-flanked, the whole
of her quivering.

Jamestown Island

15

VARIATIONS ON SOME STIRRINGS OF MALLARMÉ

1

The chest is open and I elude all the leaves
till books boil down to milk I feed you
from my virile breast this sticky honesty

you who have read all the books and left the chair
warm from your conversation   it is blue
yachts hurry up the bay strutting for the regatta

a wind from the south from the sea points the flags at me
and gulls mew   you have anchored my heart where
only everything ever comes   any craft can find me there

2

you who are blue and open and leave town   leave milk
behind I learn to drink   anchored to your conversation
my heart learns the craft of honesty   my virile books
try to pursue you   strut their sticky language

and try to be a chair for you to sit in   let me be somewhere
for you   let me everything   let me be a yacht to hurry
us to the south where we can come   face the wind
with our warm chests and read the flags of yachts

that find us in the elusive regatta of our breasts

3

to share is trust at last and I've loosed all the leaves
full of our base habit to deter the coming thing
or know its half-lit shape   sybilline   unclean
in grunted prophecy   sphincter-thrilling guesswork

16

at least o love is generous and makes   anxiety
to lure your history into my republic rich as cheese

come out and fake a yard for us to walk in   rose over bramble
vine over periwinkle   such gardens are consummations
like a couple climbing a hill and finding the sea

4

Suppose I breathed nine breaths and on the tenth
exhaled suspiring your name   yielding on the breath
the fastened image of you I hold all the time

would that nomination   which is always a letting go
reach you where you pal around a fervent city
and tell you no kind of farewell but specify

clear as my breath on your face that simply far
a friend obsessed with you is calling your name
godlike even to create a world in which you answer him?

Jamestown Island

17

And you there far away on the mnemonic lawn, what linguistic operation can rescue you now from the monolithic habits of our long deferred reality: street, table, bed? Your unexamined cunt tingles with flowers. Yet in the flash of your soft white thighs inside the penumbra of your skirt I see only the bright hard flowers of heraldry. And heraldry I also love, to turn through tricked lions and unpurchasing bezants, adoring with my eyes the sure system of their flawless self-absorbed referentiality. They too, white roses on black shields, have made me cry out in the night as you used to, though I knew no name to call them, though my body did not convulse with its own ether churning to be one with your animated stuff. Only language calls you up, starting with your name, your divided glance, the warm half-sincerity of your attentiveness, your thirst for being taken seriously but not too much. Your name with which my swart qabbalahs have not been idle. So you have become a choice emblem and a far skyline, a karmic defeat. How dare I remember? You are traveling into your own age, and presently real space will shift the stage-settings of your noncommittal passions. Why dont I let geography and aging take care of you, why dont I let lethal time unremember your hyacinth hair? Already the bloom is off your difference, and your ambitions divide you from your work. Already there broods a certain greeediness in your face that may be time or may be my eyes' revenge on you for not loving me. You are the one to whom my memory cruelly returns, and anger analyzes anew all our failed diagrams.

I am not sure what I mean when I say "not loving me." No surer than if I said "loving me." What does it mean? Let's find out. There is an obelisk in a garden. It is inscribed with a long enigmatic text in Renaissance Latin. It congratulates itself for being wise and hard to understand. It is satisfied with itself for being graceful and tricky. Moss discolors the last few lines, for lines they are, of verse, hexameters—these always hint, or even enact, a graver portent than the words in their ordinary syntactic order would connote. For the hexameter is a dance measure and shifts the words around quick or stately; *flebilis actu* is a phrase at the end of one line the rest of which is mossed, and *Nuda recedens* begins the last line of all. I fancy some bare nymph with haunches like yours, sauntering one last time into

18

the underbrush while her long-attendant satyr, I, relents at last from following. There is nothing to follow. Having you is no different from wanting you, he thinks. It, whatever it is, is here. There is an obelisk, soft Italian alabaster, soon weathered, lichened. The satyr embraces the shaft, leans on it, the hairs of his beard, some of them, get caught briefly, prickingly, in the crannies of the lettering. He thinks of masturbating on the column, letting his copious opalescent come spurt in its five diminishing spasms over the letters, further effacing the text but making it briefly gleam with its ancient luster. Ancient means former. He decides against it. He releases the stela and rests in the grass. No nymph, no tears. In an old garden there is an obelisk. Bees have nested where the base leaves room beneath it into earth. They might be hornets but he hopes for honey. He sprawls on the grass and despises his, my, long-familiar imagery: haunches, text, erasure, underbrush, nymph, stone, vanishing. Long-*known* but not familiar, never part of his family. Can he work honey from the crumbling rock? Beestings are not the issue—one pays for one's mnemonic pleasures. Why did I never take hold of you, persuade, insist, ravish? What nymph of my own distaste flees always in my meadows ahead of the ostensibly ardent satyr of my will? Is your standoffishness at last the mirror of my own failed commitment to our tryst? Because I could live without you I am without you. Never my mistress you mastered me a while. Maybe I still am mastered by the images and emblemwork of your ever-veiled identity, mastered by the *gaia sembianza* of which you once were owner and reluctant dispenser. You led me out from my marriage, and for that I'm still grateful, though it was not with you I celebrated the sacrament of divorce by which I was late initiated into my own manhood—an ardor of daily acts and daily choices, nightly stalwartnesses and sanguine alones. You let me choose, but gave no room for choices. It all was romantic but the rock crumbled. From the rotted stone where it touches acid earth (pines and cypresses are not far) buzzing sounds, the maybe-bees of my fond imagining.

Because I am rosicrucian I have left
you free to amble into otherness.
I seal my dark eyes beneath thornless scentless roses
composing lucid images in shade.

But there is a nation of which I am ambassador (as once you were a legate to me from a region of unlikely bliss). And in my real enough country I offer you asylum when you have finished with imagery and deceiving. It all is striving there and dailiness and after dark the fleshly psalter comes to be intoned. Nothing is nice. It all is sharing and being known, hence scary. Like any ambassador, I can at any moment be betrayed by events back home, find my policies rebuked, my invitations cancelled, my brief withdrawn and myself summoned abruptly back to an ominous interview with a foreign minister whose name I've never heard. But meantime for what it's worth in this contingent (hence blissful) universe, I offer you black wet wood and strict argument, a hurried landscape, conscious cities full of diligent workers, texts accumulating, unforeseen revelations, serious caresses, archaic levity. Not structure but discourse, to be succinct. And this offer is by no means exclusive; it is a printed invitation and with the ink still wet when it comes into your hands. Once I would have told them to send chariots and horsemen to escort you, and a Nubian boy with no function but to feed you raisins as you rode. Now you'll have to make your way alone, on foot, steadily doubting journey and goal. You'll have to get through the gate alone. My name will mean little to the borderguard, and he will pretend to check yours on some list. There is no list, or if there is, he has never seen it and I've mostly forgotten its distinguished names. I thought I saw your name there once, but it may have been a wilful misreading through ivy-light of some once-elegant carving on an Italian column I came across in a savage garden.

UBIQUIST

He'd be as weeds
contrive an everywhere
where any every is a fact of law
as cats are surely shallow
footed as our elms
have passed sand relents
his sculptured footstep under waves

take him out and there's just air
earth fire and initiation
luster of being wet inside
it is clear that morning is a job
to rescue moths lured by porchlight
out on errands send now
some leaves in wind
a deaf-mute alphabet he reads

only invitations to
notice of proximate arrival due
look in the book to find the stars
look for music in the bell
this scholarship is earth confusion
given in a lust of giving
answerable only to the Coming Race

incendiary lunacy all night
try to arsonize damp earth (the coming race!)
and make it radio the neighbor stars
by dint of geometric fugues
numeral inventions bare tunes
that wake the dead instead
of summoning his mind's children who
will do the work he's bound to fumble

Come help me realize my work
so that smaller is to larger

as the larger's to the sum of both
and in this rapt proportion bring to term
a pregnant poem conceived upon a word
that means "someone who wants to be everywhere."

When the brokers were raining on Wall Street
their soft knobby bodies hitting the pavement like news
I too was travelling towards the earth.

Slower, looking around, I saw explorers
decipher Mongolia, watched the men who would be my uncles
swill fat new beer in public, watched Nazi lunatics,
saw Ethiopians dying, Yeats addressing the senate,
Artaud running around Paris in magical circles, a small
man in the Australian desert was singing to me.

I couldnt make out the song, he moved bones on the sand
I couldnt understand. James Joyce read to Lucia—
I hurried to this condition where such sense could be made
and saw him sip green wine at evening. But a small
man in Australia was singing to me. I tried

to understand, I could only read his hands, I took hands
for my own, I took voices, I moved one last time like a lord
finding my mother's face. I listened,
I took bone, I let myself down in summer rain over Brooklyn
into the empty continent between the two musics I heard.

Nothing was speaking but the bones of her face.

In the house. Under the porte-cochère. In the vestibule. On the parquet. On the Bukhara drugget. On the stairs. At the alabaster lamp with the ruby-glass vane. On the landing. On the taupe broadloom. On the steps. On the uncarpeted stretch of the upper floor. In the hallway. By the bronze bust of Minerva. Her left nipple. Up the hallway. By the locked door to the tower stairs. By the gateleg table with three old magazines. By the ladderback chair with rush seat unraveling. By the framed sampler. By the dusty oil of a small lake in winter. By the window with the long white uneasy organdy curtains. On the thin carpet. By the door. In the doorway. In the room. In the room.
In the room by the window. At the garden indistinct. At the sky without moon. At the other window. By the other window. Wall of the house. In the room. On the thick rug. By the dresser. By the knob. In the drawer. In the hand a handkerchief. In the hand. In the room the hand. In the room. On the rug beside the bed. Beside the bed. In the bed. Chenille. On the bed. In the bed. In the room in bed. In the room in the bed. Superstition. In the window. Mirror. In the mirror a window. In the window a mirror. In the bed.
In bed with the room. In the hall. On foot. In the hall. In the house. In the room in the house.

Notices darker form move
against dark treey background.
It's not on all fours
therefore has language.

He prepares to speak to it
of love or knife or wine.
It is one of his kind
he fears and desires.

A joker in the endless pack,
a shape. Notices form is further.
Call back or hope go?
What words are in the mind

of the dark going one?
To know that word would be sweet.
Moves towards it to intercept
soft as if by chance.

No change of speed. No word
to need. The lines
are not going to meet.
Loses sight of figure in the woods.

Waits. Makes up conversation.
Answer to no possible question.
Asks it. Stands. Geometry
is unreliable. Lover.

Seek out the far capillaries
for instance in the fingers where

through skin you flush with color
you can touch the other universe

that reaches out its hand
to sample yours. Think

how the blood cell in its passage thinks
past and future what for us is present,

faintly conscious of its movement
down this arm. All its times are now.

So I sit in a white room at noon
knowing that no one can escape me.

It is a matter of defining love
so that time itself takes cognizance

and sings through my weariness and loss
How can you grieve? She is somewhere.

RIVERBOAT

I am a new face that joins the ship
minus the dock. When the river
sees the passengers it remembers
sudden appointments with a consoling ocean

to *there*, where nothing distracts
the self from unselfing. This
is a doctrine closed to man, who must be self
poor suicide if he remembers

every silvery detail. His heart too's
the gold mouth even the dumbest of us speak
a final answer with every single day,
eating and gainsaying. We are news

and read ourselves. But what of this river
freezing and thawing bearing sewage south
into the unimaginable sea, questioning
the suicide's elusive courage: how

to leave this place when yet one flower is
or there are lovers not mean to one another?
The river boat goes on and on, gamblers
and Melville's trickster, musikanten

and their self-esteeming din, o my the dang
fuzz bang of democratic guitars!
We see great Karnak on the eroding banks
shimmering in heat haze, the measures,

the measures. I want to keep my purity,
that tangled rope my mother gave to me
now tarred and kelp-snarled but I still
can feel along it the grit of true direction

fingering the tricky loops. By light

I steadily confuse it but by touch
I know the sensible domain towards which
I and boat and river meekly tend

north with the sanguinary flow. Nile now.
Torch on bows less to light the way
than warn our ultimate masters up there
we too are coming. The men we must become.

A boatload of pure people in shoddy clothes
full of arrogant guilt, loud with self-pity,
by inert quarrels and interrupted sleep
on self's own unearthly power makes its way.

The steam is up, sleek leathery hippos dive,
our books scatter on the decks like gulls
and Seth's hot wind brillos mauve necks
of overanxious travellers. In the saloons

they play poker and smoke ganja
and talk about their intimate relations
with a tender circumspection that brings
tears to my eyes—as if anybody's story

were different! as if any love
were not every love! Every touch
is of the pressing earth we sluggishly flee,
always bounded by what we pretend to be leaving.

So it's always river, river, not the sea.
Cunning trickery of Nile, and as for Jordan
it heals only those who lose themselves
across it in orphan comforts of the desert,

that other ocean the barren land. There
at the edge of sight corroded hills
tell the same story as our hopes:
how there was this man who to be true

to what he felt and what he knew, took
one day down in the jungle this hopeless boat
and still is faring, friendship after friendship,
into the everlasting mouth he guesses

will hold him like a stainless kiss
just between the river and the sea. Delta
of her yielded delights always he remembers.
We are instructed all day by angels

or who are they who swoop past midship
crying in the clangor of the dinner bell
and pattering like stewards' feet at midnight
outside the cabin where one more mistake

less urgent than others is just about to touch
tangle and take-off into the silencing despair
those who prematurely know fulfilment
before their wits are sharpened by keen need know.

Somewhere in the mists of what we pleasure through
knowing no other way there is a way and where it goes.
Sometimes news comes back from those who reach
and tell there is no dissolving there, no sacrifice

but only the foundering boat on a shoreless sea
and that is the surprise. We never lose them,
those companions; beside the hull
the corpses of the suicides obstinately float

and they too will reach the sea and they too
will sail across it till the sense they make
equals the sense they float in and the journey ends
and only the gaudy courtcards of the gamblers

float back to tease the next ecstatic pilgrims.

THE CHOOSER AND THE CHOSEN

There was a humid woman
in love with battle. With her crows
nestled in her lap she watched
the trying and the dying

down there beneath her hill.
She was fair of skin and dark of hair
and delicate alchemies of red
flushed her cheeks at single combats.

All round her dead
soldiers' pale ghosts settled
like scraps of paper on the grass.
But they could speak;

a voice between rainfall and a scratchy
pen and one of them said:
Lady for whose amusement we
have fought our way past being,

explain the meaning of our birth, our quick
passage, the violence for which love
was only a sort of training school,
lady, tell us why we ever were!

I am here because men think
they die for me, she said,
I am the meaning of your fall.
I am just a thing like you that feeds the birds.

You get to topple and pass on
to wherever it is the beating of your blood
concealed from you with its noise —
you get somewhere or to quiet nowhere,

I sit here forever watching your beauty torn.

EXCALIBUR

"I said this prayer to draw your love"
the lover said as he waited by the lake
for the tepid waves to part and up to come
the cold steel wielded in her hand,
the blade meant for him before the world
that only she could give. She was a woman
and he valued her as instrument,
surrounded with soft hollow words
that made the main words of her sentence
resonate, hold in place, apply to him.
As with her sword, when his, he would
cut the North Wind in ribbons and from those
airy strips weave intelligential cloths
to wave as flags above the singular peace
where all his busy thoughts held quiet
and all his complex desires
looked just like her shapely simple arm
lifting wet to him from the dark water.

ABRAK

It is caught as far as death in a mountain.
After that it is easy and the stone, jagged with release, cracks
along its axes and the bird—blue as fish glue, dim as daylight,
quick in weather—hurls its stiff wings into this ordinary life of
                                                                    ours
that is its eternity.
                    Now this instantaneous arrival of a new
organism right out of the middle of things,
                                        the way that is the bird
flies right out of the Middle Point into the you know and I know
only too well up is
                    exactly what Sappho meant in the oldest
poem when the Goddess of Love is borne to her from heaven
in a god-gold space-capsule yoked to strong stubby-winged birds
                                                                    like
sparrows too horny to fly much.
                            Creation is from the interior and
                                                                    from
this egg of inward, Love breaks out all her items in a rush.

                                    *

Rapt inly faces out the persephontic egg
grinning gold in the yolk—the horse birds hurry, horsy
hug my furry arms horsy hurry into the nursery of space
we are infant in your arrival, your cracked porcelain
our first word *Abrak* it breaks, *abrak* the walls fall, *abrak*
my horsy comes it is a girl it is a tiger too, the single leap
to be flesh consumes the finally trivial distance.
From nospace bursts into space with a cold morning sound like a
                                                        horse's breath.

                                    *

32

Crying *Abrak* the wall releases. Crying *abrak* the new beast
comes to be me. I am thick with coming.
Then the other thing, the mercy, or the long
dream goes on behind the tapestry of day,
resumes at its own pleasure, a draught from dream
blows through the evident.
                              What
kind of music is that? *Abrak* folksongs, *abrak* rock
the kind you find inside the broken egg.
You eat it or it flies away. Then long after
when it has guided you to a significant
branch on a bewildered tree
                              you take both branch and bird.
Everything that happens takes its sense from you who happens it.
You go down together.

TUNE

(listening to Benjamin Boretz play)

A sheep was. And a purse dangled from his arm. A sporran jogged between his lies. From out this pouch a cloth uncluttered, spills a spent candle and a saved penny—these to the grass. And around what let fall he graze. The relation is simple, a reciprocal. A window lets light in. The other side of the equation is the sheep. Say a sheep. Say a sheep at Stonehenge. Say a single limiter of a square wave. Say a jagged amazur, a smooth alcalde, a black pot full of juice. Say a bar-barophone and a literal linguist meet at the club. Say one is a sheep what do you say. Say to a shorn sheep what the wind shames to? A sworn sheep in a true time, by counsel led and his brief pleading, let me speak your cause, remented animal, who from the dip think deeply and the poor night foretell, joseph on joseph, fat counsellors and lean pharaoh. Fadeout is funk no more. I span and you delve, so I win and you more-than-kiss my wed feet. I am a pale bride and I clutter your home with my compunctions, nightly conceive, a bleak bird hops in and I proffer. My feet to your case. My fact to your face. Kiss me. The seat is wet from all his lies. A sheep is. Simply a sheep is, that's how it goes, is, a sheep is. The might of the silliest animal means us. Plafond. The funds of the nephew (deepest form nephew) hunger in Unc's bank. She woke "humping the bed" from a hope of other she heard singing the whiles. Have a try, deceit of musical. Heart? Have a cart. Might? I was the sheep, my full wool wet I run run between your legs you know it well. I run through you in this way, by hope incarnate dewsome in your interfact. Let me be your piece of cloth. A piece of cloth. Clad and clutter, bleed and better, "difference be-tween listening and really hearing," mouth-open one drowses—this reception is musical, is it? We had a band to the opening, lots of leap and a hallful later. A tight swaddling sort of sound would calm a lit-tle lamb. But a tight sort, a probing sort of impertinent closeness, is it? Say a sheep under Stonehenge. Is this the sun you meant to mime so long ago, its animal rising and sullen song where your eyes are on it, are lifting up with it and perception is a take-off, holding pat-tern and arrival all jinxed into one? Might? I revise the animal. How do you listen? I hear with my hands.

34

Between two birches
I walked
and it was entering
I was doing

so pallid gate
beside the road
that led
across deep fallen leaves

between two birches walked
into a country
whose only
gate is
white under saffron leaves

and I was there
in Two Birch Country
where lovers tremble
and their outlines shimmer
as they walk through air
between stone buildings and the woods
through deep fallen saffron leaves

and have been all day there
into night
two birches
flank me
as I sleep
secure in the land
where the two birch trees go.

THE NATURE OF METAPHOR

A man rises from the toilet in a public bathroom. He flushes, and begins to do up his trousers. His waistband is closed but his fly still open when the toilet begins to overflow violently. Horrified by the sudden upwelling of the primordial and irresistible flood, he rushes out of the bathroom into the corridor. A woman is standing there. She sees this man with gaping fly apparently hurrying towards her. Horrified by this primitive and menacing energy, she runs out of the building gasping. Outside, a man sees a woman escaping in obvious terror. Disheartened by the primal fear of a frightened woman, he runs away, away from her and from whatever she is escaping. As he runs, a girl on the sidewalk looks back over her shoulder and sees this agitated man rushing at her. Horrified by the primal threat of rape and aggression, she runs down a side street. Several women are walking in her direction, but perceiving her evident alarm, they wheel about and flee before her. A child playing at the curb sees the women running towards him. Horrified by this primal incursion from the realm of the mothers, the child runs for his life. He runs until he can run no more, then sinks down sobbing under a bush, among the green myrtle in the north corner of the little park in our neighborhood.

I want to tell you why husbands stop loving wives
there is a tearing
always a tearing of our hearts
into the geography of Projection
and what is most close to us must
always be found out there
                        and when the wife
is a valve of the husband's heart
and he cant really tell
her cunt from the pie on the table and the sweet
filmy curtains dancing in her windows
and all is one lovely lovely landscape
of intimate dailiness then
Christ stands up in his heart and says Get out
of her, *lech lecha,*
what is most intimate
is already you and you
must find her outside again
for a man must leave wife and father and children
to follow the Me that is himself
through the fervid gethsemanis of adultery
up the bleak hill of divorce.
And night after night the husband
hears that in his head or his heart.
Let this cup pass, and let me drink
always from the warm brown coffee mug she gave me,
let my hours count themselves her servant
and let her stand at the door at nightfall
reclaiming me back from the abstract day.
Let me love this woman
for I love her as I love my life.
And the harsh Christ of the heart says That
is why you must leave her. For every
man who studies to save his life
will lose it. And he
is implacable. The husband

in secret agonies of fantasy
sees her betraying him, sees himself
betraying her with all of her friends,
waitresses, stewardesses, actresses,
anyone at all. He speaks shyly
or she speaks shyly
of other loves and open marriages
and all the bandaids that fall away
night after night and the wound
speaks in him again. He hurls himself on her
desperate to ignite his own passion
to love her once more as he did when she was other.
But his head is turned wrong way round.
He loves where they have been and where they are.
He does not love her future.
Long ago he stopped knowing his way into her dreams
her secrets her subtle rhythms of self-disclosure.
They have feasts. They have friends.
They talk about children.
She knows it all. She has always known it
and pieces her day together from the merest signs.
For Christ talks in her too,
a Christ who wants her for her own:
woman, you belong to no one;
I gave you sun to be continuous
and night and rain
and you need no more.
They all have voices, they all
have arms. To belong
to him is to belong to society,
to Caesar—is that what you want?
And sometimes it is what she wants:
that it all could be done once for all
and life a gentle long echoing
of her first shy assent. But the voice
that hounds her says
Look at him—he brings
hardly the half of him to your bed.
He loves you too well, and you

have become landscape: Even your storms
are common in his well-known sky,
like a thunderhead heavy, handsome
over the brow of his own familiar hill.
You belong to your contract
as he does. Nothing
but what *I* do is done only once.
Everything else is again.
Die to each other and live.

POSTCARDS FROM THE UNDERWORLD

for Lisa Katzman

1

In that country there is a heap of millet
by the side of a road you have to pass

the rain does not wet it and each
passerby must nick one
and only one seed from the pile
and swallow it unchewed
disturbing as few as he can of the other grains

some of which will inevitably fall
and those that fall
slide into the human world and are born as human souls
with all the business of finding bodies
ahead of them

and he whose finger dislodged them from the heap
has them on his conscience until they in their turn
pass by the mound of millet and make their choice

Far up the road the original eater
feels an unaccountable relief
a wind springs up and parts
what he thought all along was the blue sky
and whips its veils open

and he hurries into the next country
feeling the soft spring wind on his soft throat.

2

In that country there are of course no children
and animals have to do what children do

40

look at us with pleading eyes
demanding the vastness of our comprehension
and ask to be listened to word by word
with respect both for the words they force out
and for the meanings they cant always
quite get into their mouths

It takes a long time to listen
but they are patient and walk beside us
or even sometimes carry us on their backs
always talking, telling the curious facts
of a landscape that seems to us preposterous

even after their explanations
make us think there's more here than meets the eye
the waterfall that is one long word
the blue-leaved trees from which numbers grow
the sandpits that are sacraments
where we, seemingly misguided by the beasts,
have to thrash around and flounder and feel

crystal by tiny crystal the touch of each thing
until we are worn smooth and quiet

and then they leave us nowhere in particular
and we look around and find nothing
then bed down for the night under some bush

and in the morning they are there again
telling and questioning

until we have disgorged everything we ever knew
and weary with forgetting come to a river.

3

In that country there is a river that flows north
and happy the traveler who finds it

the reeds listen to him and whisper
how he can take them and bind them
and make a reed-raft to float north on

As he floats in the swift stream he will notice
on both banks the forms of people
he thinks he recognizes
but let him not stop to enquire
or kiss again some mouth he has already worn out
with real or imaginary caresses

even the mountains he sees should not hold his interest:
he is a man alone in a boat
and what intelligence he has
should be devoted to the physics and poetry of rivers
their names and forms and behavior

let him study water
and listen only to the personless remarks it makes
he hears at the back of his head

or let him lie on his back and look at the sky
the stars are not those he knows from nights on earth
and if any of them look familiar
let him look again.

4

In that country there is a legend
that two people went hand in hand or at least
with elbows sometimes touching
down the scary stairs that lead to the frontier

Together they crossed the line and drew
wool over the eyes of the borderguard
or bribed him with beauty or poetry or blank looks

and he let them go on in
and there they are to this day

wandering in the intermittent darkness
thrilling each other with every shadow
they make out to be monster or chimera

Whereas others say they came down together
and crossed quickly to the opposite shore
where there are horrors enough
and came through the terrors and passed
still together, still hand in hand or elbows
touching or one's hand against the other's huckle,

and as they went they could be heard talking
telling each other the view from one another's eyes
which always were different:
where he saw a tiger she saw a burning furnace
and when she saw a cloud he ducked to avoid a great hand
that smote from the absolutely empty sky

with these comparisons they made each other cheer
And a third version tells that they went home together
back to the ordinary city up there
and went their separate ways
but the link between them was strong whatever the distance
and when he would see for example a burning house

he would say of his friend She is reading a book.

                    5

In that country there are groves of paper
where every traveler must stop and write
the story of his life up till that minute
when the first leaf flutters to his hand

the fewer the words the better
or he'll never finish—
it all has to be there, the nursemaid's pantyhose,
the lion's eyes, the meeting on the stairs,
the midnight ride to White Plains,

even the thing he did in the elevator.
The paper knows. When he writes lies
they dont take hold, the ink
slips off and falls along his leg,
a shameful stain that lasts a few days.
Only the true story stays written.

When he's finished he gets to drift the sheets
down a busy little river flowing there—
merfolk swim along and idly read them
lifting them a moment, conning, putting down.

How many years the writing takes
and nothing happens but the writing
and all the writer's heart is busy wanting!
But those wants won't write down.

6

In that country there are graves
from which voices plainly call at times
words that the pilgrims hear and understand—
nothing unclear about them

except what they mean
talking about hydrants and folios and Golgi bodies.
and vintages and topgallants and germanium.
The pilgrims sigh at all that clarity
wasted on their own uncultured ears.
One of them says: Nothing
I ever did prepared me to be of use;
now the words are simple burdens
carried till they fall of their own weight

leaving me light to go on
and find my own grave somewhere
where I can lie a thousand years and babble
what no one else will understand—

private I kept myself and private I lived
and the words I mouthed then in my prime
were charged with my own meanings
textiles colors fleshes phone numbers sighs.
I knew that every word meant someone I loved or feared
and the strength of my feeling eroded
all of the word except the sounding shell

and that's what I hear now, and what I'll say.

7

In that country there is a woods
and in the woods a glade
and when the traveler stumbles into it
through the last tangle of bramble and bracken

what had seemed an empty clearing
suddenly fills with all the human beings
he carries with him in his head or heart —
every one.

The field is thronged with them, they leap or lie
or rush towards him waving their attributes
all the props and clothes they wore inside him
public intense and visible all at once.
Does he deal with them?
He passes through them
as all these years they've passed through him
endlessly cycling his poor unprivate mind.

It takes a long time
so long that some say no one has yet come forth
from that field of folk

but when he does finish knowing and lingering
he steps into the woods again
moving light and elegant, no one
inside him now but himself.

45

8

In that country there is a kind of butter
that makes you think it's later than it is.
They spread it not only on the crusty bread
but on the road too and the rocks
and when the pilgrim slips and slithers his way there
finally it is still only morning

no matter what he thinks.
Everywhere there are stairs going down
and when he slides down them
there is a country where there's another kind of butter
and lots more stairs
all going down.
There is never an end of going down.
After a long time the pilgrim eats some butter
tasting his fingertip behind the grease.

9

In that country there is a door
they stand before
looking to the right and to the left
the jambs are birchwood and the lintel
is oak in which a word is gouged
that means Pass under me

It is the only word in that place
and the traveler having read it once
obeys or disobeys but does not read again.

10

In that country there is a woman
who leans against a door
the pilgrims come and watch her body
from various angles
watch it make contact with the wood

or stand away
watch the contours of the light
let between her body and the wood

and by these signs if they are signs
they interpret where the door goes
and when it will open to let them in

some of them wearied of this investigation
or their own interpretations
sit on the grass and watch the woman
hoping her face will teach them
by a sign even they cant mistake

they sit around the doorway and braid flowers
if there are flowers at their season
or else study the lady and her interpreters

as from time to time some pilgrim
looking no way different from the others
stands up or walks up
politely elbows past the woman and goes in.

11

In that country there is a pool
where travelers fresh from dying wash their wounds

they bathe and feel renewed
and go on with their excursion
their skin healthy and intact

but the pool if you look down there
through the lucid quiet water
is full of wounds
bloody intricate and rich along the bottom
like the map of any human country.

12

In that country there is a telephone
from time to time atop a wooden fence
or hung on the side of a willow tree

its purpose is uncertain
but travelers weary or benighted
sometimes pick it up and listen

they feel the familiar contours in their hand
so like a fruit you cant eat
but the phone feels strange to them here

and the feeling in their hand is stronger
than anything the phone tells them
though they listen to the comforting dial tone

and sometimes punch the buttons
and even wait for the ring to be answered
by one of those voices who answer

who speak the same maddening language
which is all you ever hear down here
you cant make out a word of it

though it all sounds just like english
spoken quickly and sincerely
in a room a little bit too far down the hall.

13

In that country they have a kind of truck
that scours along the road and lifts the dead

for they have dead men too
who fall sudden under trees or in the gulleys
and no one knows who they were in life
and no one ever saw them living

and here they are dead undecaying just dead
under some bush and the pilgrims
step over them with a shudder
or crossing themselves for fear of such
a pointless sort of condition
lying there like a sign meaning nothing

so the truck carts them away
to a place where they are brought back to life
or given life maybe for the first time
and set to walk
out under the oleander and by the waterbrooks

saying no more than they did when they were dead
but looking around with their quiet eyes.

14

In that country there is a stone that's always cool
popular at noon with those who must
walk their business along the unshadowed way

they rest their heads against it
and their hands
but the heat of their bodies does not harm the stone
(it stands as high as a very tall man
and is broad enough so that ten men
can cool themselves at it at once
talking about the weather)

but after that stone there's nothing more
for six days travel till you come to a ravine
cutting straight across the desert

down there you find shelter
down there you find a way to go
down there you find a boat

and it takes you after a while
to a place from which no messages come

though after several days silent naked men
trudge up the riverbank
dragging the same old black boat back.

15

In that country they drink wine
and take their time over every little thing
they read so slowly that the birds
lay their eggs and fly away before a page is turned

but how they read! they drink the word
by word and milk the sentence dry
of all its turnings
as if the text before them were a host of human lives
each with its options and its risks
each person threatening every day to turn
into other people

the wine clears their heads it seems
and leaves them free for birds and sluggish things
and the bookless young man who joins them
and takes them on a story with him
down through the valley and into the plain

and they remember nothing of what they've read
nothing but that there's always a chance

a river and a chance.

16

In that country there is travel inside travel
and those who all day long keep moving
dream at night of taking cruises
out into the other islands
made entirely of weather wind and behavior

for there is no weather here
only the reliable music of each place
and the only thing that happens except themselves
is the occasional troupe of marching men
who come through singing a dactylic measure
turns inside out when the travelers pronounce it:
we have come from the Holy Land
Love is the anger that knows

since they too have a Palestine a far place
where someone strove and some still struggle
to make a temple of pure talk
and one day learn to walk away from it
and die in public on a meager hill.

17

In that country there is a hoof
that comes down from the sky once in a while
and just stands there
a hoof and a slender furry shank
going up as far as they can see

they come and stand around the hoof and argue
this is Pan's foot
or this is the hoof of her cow or this
is herself's own footstep

and when the hoof is gone
disappearing sometimes in the middle of their talk
it leaves a crater filled with milk

each drinks from it or abstains
in accordance with his nature and beliefs
about the nature of the hoof

the milk tastes like any milk
somewhat sweet and flat and when
night comes it shows the moon clearly
bobbing on the pearly surface like a nervous mouth

18

In that country they have no need of flowers

but when the petals fall they cry
"It is Machine again
crying out for our attention
which is the oil we give it
                              look
at the red petals look at the mauve
purple-rimmed petals withering on earth

look and turn away"
                              There is another
part of Machine that needs them
blank sky and rootless water

air howling for any human consonant
to lick it into sense

there it is unabashed that the world wants us

but such a world it is
we hurry through it or will hurry
eyes to the ground amidst all the brightness

hungry for one dark door.

19

In that country there is a blue fire
completely blue flame
that burns low but bright
all over an immense plain

moving there you see shapes of big slow beasts
whose thoughful talk
makes the flames rise and fall or the flames
talk them
                    it is not certain

elephants and large cats
animals that might be those words
that move just past the edges of the mind
when the travelers are trying to talk

to get their descriptions in order
before they climb
up the mountains out of the weather
up to the huge cool flowing sun
unfolding sentences made of light.

20

In that country there is a wall
that works like a church
someone every morning hangs
strings of hot peppers from it
dried in the sun like old prayers

pilgrims count them as they pass
or finger them gingerly
saying:
      "This is something
      I used to know

people ate them
hung them in the sun and watched
evening imitate their color and go down

I used to eat I used to pray
but now this wall follows
wherever I go"

What is the earth that we can do this to it
like a boy with paper and a black pen?

21

In that country there is a flowering tree
round which deep rooted tawny woody plants
prong up almost leafless
                              their heads

dense spiky purple
                        these
are cut and those who cut them
point the roots at one another
and mumble what they think are spells

they read the words subconsciously from
the petals on the big tree above them
so large they hardly notice it
and the language of that tree
focused by the sap-exuding root
casts a *walking sleep* on the victim
in which he moves and works and loves and dies
for years sometimes

then comes to himself again beneath the tree
with a sticky piece of wood in his hand.

22

In that country there is a wind
and travelers walk upright against it
cupping their cigarettes in cold hands

everyone smokes there because the air
is so heavy with jasmine
that even the squirrels are languid and the birds
coast along the smoky air

and though it is not much a cigarette
is a little fire
a little choice one chooses
to inhale, not just the weather

and the wind is full of magnolia and it is always spring
and in the land of the dead one's own
death is precious
one guards it with cupped hands inhaling
this chosen chancy dwindling bitter flower.

23

In that country they have pear trees
that grow between the houses and the shore.
No one lives there, no one eats the pears.
A house, like a fruit, is a person
on a different evolutionary track.
Sometimes at night or when it's raining
a traveler sneaks into a house —
he sits in all the chairs, stretches out
over every bed. He is excited.
He cools his cheek on the plaster wall and waits.
There is no one to wait for but she comes.

24

In that country they have a distance
that fits between two people like bread in a toaster.
They still can see each other, still can talk.
But the distance is there. They feel
like different cities in the same country
or different countries in the same world.
One wakes up and finds the other gone.
But the distance is still there. He carries it
the way a blind man carries his hands.

THE HEAD OF ORPHEUS

When Orpheus walked beneath the trees
all the leaves were Eurydices

when Orpheus looked into a well
he saw the skies of hell

when Orpheus took up his lyre
he saw his funeral pyre

on which the Maenads tossed
his scattered limbs and hissed

"Everything he did was wrong:
love and theory, wife and song"

yet when they picked up his head
they kissed his mouth and said

"All the lies these lips told
kept us from ever growing old—

now keep them wet eternally."
And Orpheus saw them throw it in the sea.

ODE TO LANGUAGE

To put on shoes and be sophisticated
—it really was a creamy trumpet
Miles Davis made—or gleam waxy
and smile along the El-shadowed street
through all the synaesthesias of weary language
patient, at our command, like an old dog.

Faithful animal! Endure
Tehran, Stella by Starlight, Nautilus
machines, the skanky fantasies
of men no longer young, the rough
edge of graffiti, borrowed vices
of exurban novelists, the price of glass.

Break me. Come to me
with burrs in your fur, tell me
where everything has ever been.
Growl at me if I sleep, wake me
with your dependable craziness.
Birds plummet and you fetch them
wet from your mouth. Women weep
in San Francisco. Only you

are ever different.

1

à travers la rivière une chose

et sur la face de la lune
une chose et
parmi l'abaissement des ifs sous le vent
une chose et
sous la mer une chose
et tous la même chose

mais nos pieds marchent une autre —
et comme un garçon amoureux
s'habille en voyant
le soleil comme un texte sanglant
qu'il faut qu'il déchiffre

pour être un beau jour nu

ainsi nous déchirons
le sol sans mot
et nous ne cherchons pas l'autre

mais la même chose seulement

2

Âme où rues coulent
ayez soif pour moi

âme où rossignols se taisent
en extase blanche de rien dire

ayez soif pour moi
et quand le soir rature le jour erroné

ayez soif pour mon silence

3

plus simple parler une langue
que le coeur n'entends pas

l'habitude de tout comprendre
apprends écrire de droit à gauche

et un arbre nouveau marche

4

j'habite seulement avec toi
nos corps se soumettent à la loi
des corps — qu'une chose
s'éloigne d'une autre une distance
et cet espace est une bouche aveugle —

mais j'habite seulement
avec toi toujours avec toi
et la demeure
se lève des lignes subtiles d'un dessin
et les vitraux sont des yeux
nous nous voyons

lit, presque jour

5

Ongle à doigt:

Ne parle pas
de quelque destin imprévu

je mange l'autrefois de peau

et sous mes rêves
les corps entiers (nés
de mes caresses)

se lèvent et osent grandir

jusqu'au moment quand je m'oublie

fesses   hanches   dos   durent
je suis une lame   un minuit   je passe.

VARIATIONS ON A POEM OF STEFAN GEORGE

Windows where I once with you
At evening looked into landscape
Are bright now with a foreign light.

Path still runs from the door where you
Stood without looking around
Then curved down into the valley

At the turn once more you lifted
To the moon your pale face.
But it was too late to call

Darkness — silence — stiff air
Sinks as it did then round the house.
Every joy you took away.

1

Windows where I in selfish air
looked stiff into evening
wanting you to stay

But I was the path, the dark
valley that sucked you away
was my strange light, my call.

Everything you took with.
What is left is a joy
like a pale face in moonlight

not sure which way it looks
as the door falls down the valley,
as the door becomes landscape

and you come back constantly
along the selfish path I am
waiting at evening for your call.

2

You went and I window.
I am selfish with light
and I am stiff with calling.

I am the path where you
once turn round too late for silence
too late for moons

I am stiff as glass because the light
shows you only going out and coming back.
Come back the way a face

sinks around the house and makes it stay,
the way a moon turns
into a window and the landscape

runs from the door.

3

At evening you look in.
I am stiff with calling
and you are bright with doors.

It was too late to look around,
the joys of valleys are a silence
you took with. The turn

was where the evening door
fills with foreign joys and we stand.
We stood. Once
with you at
foreign landscape
to the moon
too late for
you curved
down into silence

4

windows where I once with door
summoned a turn in the path
and the moon looked over her shoulder

till the landscape filled with standing still
come back the way a place
becomes foreign and a door looks around

and you bend around the silence
and your face lifts in the stiff air
and veer back what once curved away.

5

Stiff in your valley
your face sinks round me
and I am bright with a strange window

6

in the land a shape I saw
since noon, too late to call
I stood in hell with framed unlight —

woe to standers! oh to have your name
to shower down in, starry light!
fate knocks loud from the door,

time bleaches anger,
a tomb to roof my spite —
jungle of glass from which we looked

I am made simple by distance.

7

and this land shape I saw
has you in it turning back
and lifting to the moon again

the foreign windows of your face
so they will shine for us,
those stars whose unlight

frames hell as a house
from which you curved away—
but now the bright silence

veers you home.

8

I am my body and I want you back
I am my body and I am my mind I
am my body and I want your mind

whatever I am I want your body
curving back to look at me
the way a face looks at the moon

and I want your moon to be my mind
and your mind to be my face and I want
to look around me and find you

I want to look up at your face
the way a window hears a house
and a door falls through landscape

endlessly opening. Then the dark
turns silent and only your name
stands in the mind of the door.

9

You turn back and see the star
that brightens with your tears.
It is a name to hold in mind.

A valley to revisit.
The mail never comes, you have
to bring it to the door.

It is always noon in this jungle —
in the darkness a silence sways,
tries, tears the emulsion of an image.

We are together — then
bleach the dark and turn
lifting again your pale face

to my body. I am your door
you are my path we are our house —
light finds your name

to shower down in once for all.

10

Moaned, and I mean you more
the want I do you turns me
to the door, to spite all calls
and still call out. To veer
towards you and leave every valley

and find you where a star *stands*.
Stall me under hedges, bright
with seeing you again I turn the path
itself into a house, the land

into a window, time to a door
and we stand together not looking back.

11

Find a star where it shines with tears
evenings in the land, shape you saw
since noon: hell with framed unlight.

Fate knocks loud from the door: woe to
standers. Oh name to shower
down in! Stall me under box hedges,

by your care warmed, no male ever
moaned. Time bleaches angers.
Thought is where to spite tomb-roofs —

jungle — swaying — starry light
sings between emulsions. A house.
All is freed, and names you mine.

12

Fenster wo ich einst mit dir
Abends in die landschaft sah
Sind nun hell mit fremdem licht.

Pfad noch läuft vom tor wo du
Standest ohne umzuschaun
Dann ins tal hinunterbogst.

Bei der kehr warf nochmals auf
Mond dein bleiches angesicht.
Doch es war zu spät zum ruf.

Dunkel — schweigen — starre luft
Sinkt wie damals um das haus.
Alle freude nahmst du mit.

ORIGINAL WOMEN

How it was in the beginning was once revealed to me.
The beginning of the human race, that is,
I know nothing before that or beyond it.
There were women.
There were no men.
Women were first and women were only.
What we call humanity was a race of women
about whose culture I know little
except that it was highly developed,
fully articulated technologically, musical, Edenic.
This land was Eden.

Watching the sexuality of animals, their two-by-twoness,
their polarization into opposite sexes,
these complete women grew interested in the possibility
of externalizing their *centrifugal component*
as a separate living being.
How would this serve them?
They began their researches, and concluded after long study
that they could externalize this component
as a sort of servant,
a clone-like creation that would be structurally adept
and characterologically eager
at doing things women felt themselves annoyed by or clumsy at:

lifting heavy weights from the ground,
throwing things.
A class of servants who would be entertainers and porters
was intended, planned, made.

And woman took man out of her own side.

By biological engineering this feat was achieved
(our distorted legends tell us of this as the "science
of Atlantis")

and she looked on what she had made
and deemed it good.
She gave it half her name
and felt tender towards it
and called it man.

She gave it language and guided its experiments,
suggested harps and flutes, sketched alphabets,
bothered it till it stored its head with rimes and numbers
and equations and the memories of celestial events,
an adept valet, a prompter, a musician to sing to her,
a man to carry her belongings.
She taught it about grains and hunting,
and left such unfocussed, time-consuming, boring tasks to it.
At night it sang to her her praises
and it has been singing since.

Then the great tragedy took place
the one that has resounded ever since in our legends:

Like masters ever after, women fell for their servants.

They fell in love with their projections
With their creation

they fell in love
they fell

it was the Fall we've all heard of
(why Eve was the first to bite the apple,
why she taught Adam to love her
why she lifted his humble eyes to look on her as a partner,
she who had been his maker and his god)

They modified men's bodies and their own bodies
so the delightful genital congruence made for pleasure
could have a procreative consequence,

they rebuilt themselves to bear children
only from the impassioned thrust of the servant —

this was their gift of love to their beloved creature,
by giving up to him
the right that had always been theirs,
of propagating by their own unaided will:

they had given him the gift of life in every sense

and man was grateful for a while

but for millennia now has tried to deny
that he was ever a servant —
his dim vestigial memories he disguises
as the relation between himself and god

and he knows the whole thing is somehow women's fault
but he does not know how

he blames her still

blames her for needing him
when deeply deeply she is absolute
and he needs, will never be happy till he admits he needs,
to love and serve her and entertain her and throw
small stones at palm trees for her to dislodge sweet dates.

[*All histories and all bibles tell this story, mostly backwards, most-
ly upside down — but this revelation I received one day six years ago
and here repeat, this revelation shows you how to read them rightly.*]

69

From the central divisions
from the middle of the Three
that shows itself as Four,
from the One
that is made or seems to be made
by the Two around it,
from the middle, from the lake
which is mother of numbers,
from the unthinkable manyness
of things in the world,
from the center of all the things
from the one building the fire left,
from the One in the heart of the Seven
from which all the textiles and numbers come,
from the colors and sizes of things, from the beast-like
undependable tameness of objects,
from clothes and soaps and tobacco,
from the One that polishes bronze here and there by its touch
from the mane of the lion, from the roar,
from the middle finger, from the lance of the Trinity,
from whatever is the center of itself,
from the ravelled thread of the buttonhole
from the shirt taken off
from the heel of the shoe and from
the shank of the shoe
worn through by walking,
from the middle, from the stride
balanced on an invisible fulcrum
each body discovers and wields,
from the pivot, from the cock
standing in soft wind,
from an empty glass, from
the silence in the heart of a story
where the teller pauses and the tale waits
poised in its molecular library
of all possibility, from the heart that is possible,

from the sureness that is doubt and the doubt that is leap
and the fall that is conviction,
from the loss that is Eden and the tears
that turn into morning.

Chicago

I want to tell you
something simple
how when we sleep
together our breath
goes somewhere
I dont know I guess this
where it must

and seems there
an ordinary air
flowers could breathe
from our two mouths
so close together
a single complex idea
they proliferate
petal by petal
until it has a single
name, like "rose" or
today the "daffodil" is
ready
        yellow
                only
the name is simple
after all
and I've told you
one more lie

tell it with me
until we can think
of something longer
than flowers
something purple
something instead

—the earth is tired
of comparisons

they live with each other
in the sky they answer Why
questions with a silky shrug
of their busy hips a smile
we are not perhaps their business
but we swim attractive in
this lake of theirs our history
and when we betray every other
for the sake of some one hour
in a musky Trojan bedroom they
notice our ardors in some
way what we do pleases them
or rimes with their vast betrayals
of everything that simply is
when they want more
the impenetrable appetite
to be what they are not to be
what the other is they turn
inside out and they watch us
bored between their tricks and take
the kind of interest in us
we might take in raindrops
dripping down the windowpane
leaving a trail of wet behind
they read as sex they read
everything as sex they watch us
do anything at all for the sake
of putting something of me
into something of you they understand
how exalted and narrow this
ambition is a lancehead
to pierce all phenomena and let
the same light in the same blood out
that is their wine too
their spermy nectar they sip from us
locked in what we think is personal

and that makes them smile too
the arrant nonsense of our souls
the raft of meaning we construct
to enterprise our pissy seas
but they have no seas no souls
nothing but us to watch
and nowhere to go but what we do
whereas we are infinite
in our confusions in our lust
we know to move in our love
we dwell our way into enduring
and in our betrayals rear huge
meaningful structures that tell
our feeble progeny Do this
make a stone stand make heaven crack
and shove your body in the rain
take hold of every slippery thing
and hold as long as you can
until the holding is yourself
and your last love is letting go.

COLORADO

for Tandy Sturgeon

Fastidious dislocations of a fugue a saturday
how does it come "my name is Monika"
"I am boring" there are squirrels in the park you
have heard it all before it is the bran of breakfast

the brass of everyday in shadow it was cold above
florentine rooftops ruddy tile the sun decked city spread
a table in shadow a radio on a mountain voicing
elytra of spring the clicky whir begins the green

"my name is Brown" now does the table with its muddy seats
feed me your body I am tired of asking but with receiving prone
I complicate your ground "her name is Brass" red squirrels
in the hills on monday time when all were working

came love into the world and we alone were citizens
the never-tired rocks the radio keeps voicing only once
confessed my longing or let it answer new material
what is clutched too hard loses wings "my wing

my wing" "my name" in shadow we had the city
and voiced it as we chose spend time with me spend
citizens of tables we are never far from money
get down expensive rooftops in your lap only one is ever waiting

or all the waiting voices become one body exquisite
dislocations of metal lattice structure what I breathe
is gold a new light share with me I am happy
in the hearing there are bands around the hills cream

light over the incessant prairie "her name is grass"
and we're here to study beetles to test the sung light
against insect ardor and carapace *musik* o friend
who sits on the table before me a dish of cream a ceremony

forgiving red animals "I am hungry too" the roofs
slide down the hill in the mauve shadows of America
tender flower unpetalling by questions "I will always
listen" "I am implied by your voice speaking" in ferns

the youth alone is eaten unpeel soft papery sheath
the beady shoots uncurl by steam there are black cars with us
African voices on the hill polite as rooftops "I was happy
I knew" something would happen your body shifted on the wood

there is no fugue like spending time with you a lesson a lap
in the frail language where the work goes always on
and we are free to study hills big balls of little squirrels red
I can admit my longing the longing is geography and speaks

all distances as relevant to that coming towards
and inside a florentine discovery green in the heart of rock
a sunset roof all noontime we bear our times easy "a
ceremony forgiving longing" "my name is looking for"

you have to love me to understand this text "a box
is intricate the inner angles of its sides and bottom
extend in space to form an alphabet" the mountain reads
African voices full of morning on the hill so cold in shadow

we we stand looking down the temple gardens blind water
history blind we bear each other's destinies and falter
under weather we are intricate "we are money" and all
voices are worth hearing "all I do is hear you" hearing

forgives animals forgive cities forgive mountains the radio
is never silent I love the machine of our bodies the table
sleeps the crowded altarstone of our condition "is that a squirrel
a pale red agate moving a fall of rock?" we are close

to the confusion of water I am elegant to be prairie
"you mistake me if you think I'll ever die" do you listen
do you forgive the machine "at your peril forget my power"
"my name is everything you hear" small city with sunny roofs

stand bent-kneed to can it be so simple to
slip inside you after all the voices intricate muscles
implying that most here we are speaking in this small mountain
without grieving meeting some people all the time the red

beneath your skin foraging for light it could be breakfast
after night's drinking loving this simple is it lake of light
and broil a fish there on this humble fire flake for you and me
"I was waiting for you" a fact is we have eaten and the bone

is chewable from fire the chemical destiny mountain loud
the radio is not tired bend your knees and hold my image
density is closest to the heart the sun of inside stories
imago flying metal spell the last name you hear in shadow.

WHAT SHE FOUND IN THE RIVER

was a piece but not of music
(was the natural Me of any husband
who will enter his wife but not possess her
save in those bitter words "my wife, my
woman" as if by that easy uneasy pronoun
could be appropriated
the gorgeous rag of her identity)

[the wife speaks:]

"I was surprised to find this in the river
you lost it fishing, you swam
after that lazy carp, she drew you
flaring her metal fins, down
into the city below any river, street
of the unborn. There you lost it,
making love to some trout-wife, some lewd
she-fish guppying along down there.
You lost it to a pharmacist's wife, lost it
in Tucson, she distilled it over steam
and set the gleety residue to burn
with awful slowness in the light of the moon
caught between two mirrors. You lost it in mirrors.
At night you milked it away, day by day
you put it in women for safe-keeping. At noon
it was nobody's. Now it is mine and I scorn it,
common common liquor, glib gift,
oil of children, god grease—on my hand
I waste it, let it glisten, let it peter out
running down the lines of my palm."

And from the grave on his side of the bed
he makes answer: "I read your palm.
Long your life is and soft your heart.
Your fate reaches past your mind.
Mercury is blank. I am your only child.
Do not estrange my solemn difference."

78

"Oh love you talk such nonsense nonsense.
You lost it and it's gone. You lost it and it's found.
It is the cream of all your seeing, a glob
of all your knowing, a silvery mistake, foam
from rapids, dreams of a drowning man,
spit from your poor blind god."

a sleepless week will not impede
twenty hours after my last nap
a formal structure from knowing itself
here (call it a garden

out of sheer ballsiness the trees
topiary the rocks confounded grots
and every stream an amnionic sluice
from which a vista's born

form form form (the house itself
wanders in the garden
and there are certain precious leaves
that medicine my life

by name! their names! (and stone
shaped like hell-mouths
shaped like fear and off below the pines
a man dressed for travel digs

with his bright spade he digs until
beneath the topsoil he tenderly uncovers
a woman sleeping naked
who rouses and steps out of earth

her eyes still closed (it is She
come to us again the loam
sifting from her breasts she moves
across the ordered path and passes

into the unordered underbrush
she is the only definite (she proves
something, that the soul will never die
that every object is transparency

(we killed her and the myth forgive us
we killed her and she returns
her side-wound clotted with flowers
spring again and things suddenly exist.

THE ARCHER

This small arrow
piercing my name
I asked Eros "How
is it that you target?
You get the names right
& the bodies wrong—
our identities
are mixed." He whispered:
"I am a torment & a worm,
a venomous waking
& a day full of joy.
I am all contradiction.
Shouldnt you, plural,
chosen by me for my own,
show the same turbulence
as churns in me & only
for one instant comes
to perfect balance when,
my bow stretched to breaking,
my arrow suddenly lets go?"

SOME PRINCE OF THE TROJANS HERE

ONE

Among the trees with names
the me's with names
there is another person

no name for that weaving

except we see pursued
from warp to weft
in bronze or naked
sometimes bleeding

whose blood stains the dry wool
a comfortable sleepy brown
beyond the mind

no name in the sleepy mind
and tragedy leaves no more trace than this

a war a place I stood in
by the altar
watching my brothers dying, my many sisters
raped or yielding

in the weaving

and I say if you ask me
I remember a book
a kind of poem
in some uncertain language
a mass of images and resentments
of things that were beautiful

something fallen, some purpose
all that dying served

beyond me, beyond me

and am I the only one who remembers?
I held my hand
I did not kill and did not rape
I said: *I am the priest of this,*

by my beauty I make sense of time
I make sense of any this

I have had so many sisters
what can the ocean do to me?

For I could cross, I thought, and keep
my pure hands and desiring mind
and found as many cities as I chose

as many cities as found me
in the wilderness beyond the book.

Then it was west.

TWO

We called him Apollo
for his bright songs, the bright
goldbeaters' work around the city,
the cast of living mind that sought
beauty in all things, all persons
and made of it our civic order.

We tried to possess him
and in our common furor he
consented to be possessed,
appeared often before us, stayed, gleaming
lord upon Tenedos

and helped us. And then

84

when it was all done
it was his measure
that gave beauty to our enemies,
his music that held together
the ballads that tell of our ruin
they sang by their brutal feudal campfires.

And we had nothing but exile
ocean and remembrance,

hyacinths in April and roses in May,
Sun that he is he illuminated
equal-handed beauty and its ravager,
city and those country squires
who pulled our walls down
and burned his altars, by fire's
blaze
      fixing his worship in the mind's forever.

THREE

But this is hearsay,

what I read in their books.
What I know is a nameless dark
full of men and women
all my siblings, all my loves
caught up in dying

and I may have died with them
and this speaking be a breed of death.

I know I travelled, or I travel,
fixing the names of places in my speech,
these places, real, no realer,
equal-handed memory!
Scamander, the bleached pebbles
of drought-stricken Delaware
under Lackawaxen, the big

85

cottonwood at Wounded Knee
where I sheltered from the centrigrade
of that same finally nameless god,
accountable, making me so also,
the drift of evidence, westward
into mere feeling.

I have the names of things, o tree book
with your colored names,
weaving I follow with my fingers.

In beauty I have come
into body
this American science

into my body born
out of language and memory
freed

and my hands
following the weaving
stretch
        among low dusty branches, blue
dusty berries of the juniper.

BINDING BY STRIKING

Say I come to you by circles. Say the line
that carries my name keeps me
from knowing you as a car knows a garage.
Say I am a wine you know better than to drink.
Say I, seeing the pale skin inside your upper arms,
become a better animal and become water.
Say this water doesnt pull but when you fall
takes you altogether in. Say you are in.

Say we sit on some steps together, or a wall.
Say something falls. I come to you then confused by lime,
sand, long hair holding the mortar together.
Say we stand a long time and one of us falls and one
catches, one catches and one lets go and it's night already.
We are still together. Say I am oily and you're dry.
Say a straight path and a twisted gate. Say something
not easy to say. Say the self-renewing knot of flesh
they call the rose blocks at times the future prong.
Say we belong to each other. Say the same thing
that holds us holds us apart. Say we struggle
to get in and stay in and not ever leave. Say for a change
you are out and I am in and I have trees too
your path gets lost in. Say you have numbers I can count
and numbers that leave me out. Say we change
but say we are always being held to the same.

Not to say little of same. Not to say one is more than some
or some less worth than every. Not to say every.
Not to say your pale skin is paler than or this wall higher.
We rise where we fall. Not to say the word that draws us
doesnt some way let us in. Not to say in is the only.
We are held where we call. We know something and are held
to what we know. We fall through the wall. Not to say
there is only one garden or one car. Not to say one
when we mean "a road" and not to say going when we mean
    "home."

87

Not to say time when we mean space. Not to say stone
when a wind blows through the place where we've fallen.

Say you come to me by line. Say the circle you understand
has more light than a bone and more air than a tower. Say
the broad leaf of burdock plays two pieces of music:
bug-holes and leaf-shadow. Say a skin is like that and that
what we have consumed gives us light and what is gone
is the constellation that guides us. Say you have come
and will come. Say the language is dry and the wall is low.
Say a word gets over the wall. Say we are in. Say my skin
draws you. Say what we do with each other goes on.

Say a voice that you hear. Say that we know ourselves
chiefly in many. The Oil of Others is the light-giving flame.
Say we are same. Say we come to it simply again.

IN MARY FRANK'S GARDEN

A leaf to be brave
to celebrate
a dismemberment a *raptus*
Proserpinae again

the beast that is a body
firm of clay & shapely
understanding the ground

I am a part of what falls

& when her legs sprawl & the small grass
comes up between her pelvis & her thighs

her skin is intricate with fern
I am an everywhere & her scattered body
becomes the wholeness that I live.

It is technical, the size
of a kiln, how big a piece can be, a part
to make whole

these myths, among the gardens
where the stones start—

I felt I was at the beginning.
Narrative flows from image; image
is a sudden sense of the body
overwhelmingly there,
                        our own made distant,

the whole becomes a part.
Flows from this garden. A habit
to heal us again, *sparagmos*

& then rememberment, the body found.

Such senses. So many bodies
nested in this one that walks, nested
in me as I am nested in clothes,
the billowing, the tight.

In the garden the body sees itself in all its parts
scattered & known by landscape into place,

description. I dont care that they
inhabit flowers or perch on the big rock.
I care that they extend me into power
& are tender, that there is so much lust here,

so many parted lips.

SIZE

for Jeanne Tooley

Jeanne, however big it is
we see it with our same eyes
& the biggest landscapes I've ever seen
—south from the Badlands over grass,
the skies of Hereford County, Texas,
Mojave—
were all just rooms
because my measure
wields them, is that it?,
& the wild rain
is like the grey sky over Bergen Street
when I was ten, in the dentist's big window,
Good Friday, scared, the light that is God
dying over a vast city.
Which is no bigger than my touch.

If we were lovers we would know
how a pair of arms takes in
every immensity & brings it to you,
yours in the act of sharing, as
to say "I have been
in Dakota, I have seen the snake of lightning
sting the huge earth
when there was nothing but sky
to hide in" is to say "Here—
it is yours
because I became it, it poured
into me & made me new.
I bring it to you."

THE LATTICE

(Alice in her lattice
allows to be nibbled
her arm by the truth)

"Is this love? Is this the train
my aunt saw smoke across the prairie
so far off she couldnt hear it but
never spent another night with Uncle Fred?"

"I have to do
all the things
she accuses
me of wanting to."

(One lattice
and it holds her tight.)

"Why is my arm so white
after so much sun? Things nibble
at me and leave no bites.
The authority of innocence is preserved.
Bend my knee. Spread my lap
to catch rabbits in my dress.
Sky-bunnies, Hegelian vermin."

Everything analyzes.
Currents of glass
remembering your last fire —
silhouettes of people like her
against bushes like me.
It's unsettling to be free.

The *golden afternoon*, the draught
between two beech trees, the flurry
of partridge wings: *get married,*
get married. These stupid

lovabilities that make her dread.
Remember.

A licit enterprise
always asking for more funds—
the money we make up.
By the fire it is August but the roof
walks over rain. There are birds
but not here. Herons, cranes.
What is delicate
cares.
This fine silk weaving I have done
twice now for you, dont
ask again, I am thin
with my weaving, thin with design, desire,
I love you with my last silk—
and do not watch me weaving.
                                        But he did.
He saw the crane she was, her breast
plucked bare of feathers, bleeding
and this blood became her weaving.

Never come back to me
always ahead of me be
waiting at the crossroads of metals
where the fur fields wave
and the animals are all machines
and this game I play
becomes the same as God.

Never comes back to me
with souvenirs of our future
never treat weather like a bird in cage
or a girl in your bed,
let it be different always
because this little river
runs from nowhere to nowhere

and sinks out of sight
while my hands are still open
and the whole wind is a crystal
I analyze by sleeping with

Never comes back to me
on roads like lively eels like
cute sentences like advertisements
never come back to me always
be ahead of the desperatest dream
kind as cream cheese silent as laundry
be the god of my house, Man,
but never come back.

This lattice I lie in
is the signature of your absence

here I make sense of your senseless name.

The language below the language,
lady, is the sense of it, the sex

how you from Cahors or you
from where the aqueduct flows out
take counsel with your laps
and then propose
a regimen of flowers, those gaudy masks

cracks in the large glass.

What is broken becomes the sex of things.

For five minutes there was feeling,
I felt and knew nothing except
that I was feeling. Nothing spoke.
Then she asked me for a word, Say
what you feel as a word. No word came,

then *Ja, Ja,* an easy, I had
no native language then, then
I just had feeling. She pressed
down on my pharynx and said Say it
as a word. And there was feeling,
silence. I am remembering. I knew
nothing, there was no thinking.

Lady of glass there was no thinking
and all these years I thought you were conceptual only,
reachable through the red & green lights of head's streets
and instead you were rain and raisins
less even than sugar, less
than bees, you were barter,

you were something that fits
in something it fits in.

What language should I choose for my discourse,
should it be the clipped laze of Venezia,
the stalwart arches, words held high off the ground,
of the Bolognese, or the Lombard blonde tongue of Milano,

can I color your hair
with any hue, can I invest
in the gold sun glints there
when we sheltered under the warm old wall
when the vines were past flowering?

I want a language of glass
fragile and permanent,
where everything that happens to me and to it
is faithfully rendered, cracks,
cracks perpendicular to cracks,
Eros's blackboard, age, craze,
a network of streets going nowhere,
to see through
a language-patterned image to you—

do you want such talk?
do these cracks align with yours?
There is a sex to these joinings,
a manifest hardon
coming towards you to be included—

She leaned forward on my chest and said Tell me
and then precisely I was silent, the sheen
of my language cracked, I gave her
my silence, my precious unanswer
and the tears flowed, I sobbed
discreetly, hated my mildness, hated
my compliance, cracked,
and then there was no hate, no sense
but sensation, nothing to feel
but feeling, nothing to be but feeling.

For these cracks are the logic of silence,
schoolroom of love.

This glass gaze this *stumme Person*
silent woman who lifts her jutting stern
proud over the frenzied air because regarded
"Oh where is my voice my prow
to slice this minnowy orchestra of wavelets
and smash myself on some proud island
equal-measured to my rich self?"

the island is a man-machine for waiting
accurate at the intersection of the cracks
dance? drama? a polstergeist rules his roost
an arrogant omphalos, a cyclops in his hand—
"this canister is packed with outer space,
I nibble you with my Uranian weather,
come home to me sleek-hocked traveller
you are a line cracked in the glass,
I am another, hence
                    you are my mother,
I feel your classical music." He says.

96

Such antics around me. They dance
through labor
and bear to light
a thirsty music.
Radio Azoth—I am the end of things.

Cloud by day
the lattice lasts

hast guided us
a spume of fire nights a cloud hand days

shepherding us
your flock

to where the dark lives
rocks soak up the honey of dawn

so you're in love and everyone looks love
and that's what the weather told me waking
the day also is.

               At times I wake near,
edge of the lattice, and see just past it
the excited instability of local light,
the light of Arcturus touching this Sun's light.

Feet, forgive street.
Hip, forgive hand.
Man, forgive game.
Woman, forgive man.

A LIFE OF INTIMATE FLEEING

Under the cypresses the air is still
the long meditations of the mosses
have gotten nowhere. Tangled in themselves
they forgot what they were thinking.
"No, we were just thinking. There is
no object, only subject, so we are
as the poem is, a nest of brackets
enclosing"

       brackets, does memory
have a *core?*

And under the cypress on drier ground
one takes off clothes,
takes and takes
and there is only clothes
one by one cast into the vanilla-scented
     gearwork, branches
of these infinitely slow machines.

From image to image
we flee by night.
It is a passion
of running.
We who live in gardens
have no point
but the next flower.
Why is it winter?
Make things and touch people—
is there another law?

2

From room to room
immensity.

An hour, by touch.
Excitement by shape
promises a kind
of knowing that is new.
And then another street.

And always the same Law.

The law a boat
the beast a passenger
we steer.

Since going is the loveliest,

and when it runs
splay-silked against the uddery wind
it also like water quivers
among the tall grasses as
if this kind of water can stand up
and shape the wind that stirs it

3

a nest of brackets
enclosing sky

fork of the great tree.

DOORS

Suppose you didnt know what a door is. That it opens, for instance. It would seem a different part of the wall, thinner, more resonant. A decorative rectangle set in the wall, an embodiment of some geometrical mystery like the Golden Section. It would seem tantalizing to someone trapped in the room—a perverse, mean tease: the wall is thin here, soft, but still unpassable. How little it would take to get through the wall, yet you cant.

Suppose you didnt know what a door is, that it can open, that its resistance defines the zone of least resistance, but that zone requires a deft use of something learned, a knack, a skill: twisting the knob and pulling. Or pushing. Even if you got as far as turning and pulling, if the door were the kind that opened outward, you'd still never guess, never get through.

Suppose all round us there are things like doors in things like walls and we never knew.

face at a window
who are you
caught
between the tangled drapes
a face looking out
at all the dark
in which I pass
sometimes lit up
by the same streetlight
that streaks
a hint of somebody I once knew
across your high round cheeks
dark eyes, dark hair
my love,
my anyone.

THE SECRET AGENT

To be what I am is to be guided.
The man at the counter beside me,
who orders what I order, or a slight
variation on it, his coffee
darker than mine for instance, he
is the one I'm here to find. Protect,
interrogate, assassinate—I dont know yet,
my mission declares itself in time.
But he's the one, always the first one I meet.
It is easy to identify my target—look
at the woman ahead of me in line, the man
on the barstool next to mine, the old woman
who asks me the time. This is the very one
I ease across the border with my skills
to disguise, impersonate, liquidate.
For a man like me the world is full of borders.
They are the veins of my true body,
this planet of distrust, this war.

THE MOUTH OF THE BLUE DOG IS BOUND BEFOREHAND

for Michele Martin

We can walk through the blue night and no blue mouth will bite us. They come here from the last place and watch the discerning gamboge of the late leaves; under such and such a tree it is good to meditate. Under such another, it makes sense to make love. Here it is dream.

I am weak before you,
true mouth.
Therefore I have bitten
your eastern lip.

Therefore I carry
this blue charm
whose words the world
improvises against

its own blue night.

Wake me. You are the first messenger I have ever been able to believe. That is strange to me, an altogether different book.

Have a horse.
(Name him.)

Have a house.
(Move in.)

So there is money in the mind, and seven bowls of pure water constantly differencing. This means. That means. All means avail.

Have a.

And then I am not. And for a while not, and for a while. Then it is a risk one way and a risk the other. Then there are two deer walking by. Then there is a mistake. Then we look and see it's only one more color.

I write home to my mother. I telephone. There is an island. This is another.

I spoke about it to the printer's representative who had come from the west to talk about it with me. I said there is a thing called kerning, and things called coppers and brassies. There are letters in words and words have spaces inside them too. Really elegant printing attends to these. Attention attends to everything. The poet worries about spaces between words and the printer to spaces between letters. Whose task is it to worry about the spaces inside sounds?

Worry?

She had no chance to be alone. The way of life in the valley was based on sharing space, a space from which each person spurred off into that private domain or mind to which they had not yet contrived public access. No chance to be alone; it was wrong, to have the daily life wholly available to everyone but the heartmind locked close. She knew it had to be otherwise, to turn that relation around. To be private, and open the heart of meditation to the whole universe.

Universe?

It is absurd to question what is transparently here.
Absurd to name it?

But is this the real difference, the shared, the closed? Is there a relation (there must be a relation) between the world lived and the world held bright in mind?

There is. It is called *what I mean*, where "I" is code for "the sum of all possible meaners."

Meaners?

It is accurate to live alone. Hot water in the morning, bread. Footstep in the grey pale mud deep in the forest, one's own. The territories inside a room, the travel. It is accurate to live alone, the bread.

They were quiet in the room. They were being alone together. One writes, one reads. One sleeps. One sleeps. One unscrews a jar and offers roasted nuts.

One?

On. Man. Impersonal. Not the self, that Worrier.

But who gets the typography straight then?

The trees. Bare, almost all of them bare. And back there, on the lowland under the bluff, between it and the bay by the river, there are hardly any evergreens. Oak saplings holding their leaves long, the curled dry yellows.

Who goes there?

You are the first messenger I have ever believed. It is hard to understand. *Stong-pa-nyid.*

It is all there is to understand. The first, the voice.

There is a picture of an old woodblock print, a talisman against dogbite. It shows a dog, a chain, a symbol that holds the one to the other. Every talisman implies a system, ratifies it.

In the wilderness those who walk alone at night fear the watchdogs of the occasional settlements they near. Those dogs are big, fierce, cannot distinguish pilgrims from thieves. Perhaps the distinction eludes them, rather, or strikes them, known, as inconsequential. (As it might strike a thief as irrelevant whether the dog that bites him is blue or red.)

The teeth close on what I take to be my leg.

All beings need a charm against this bite.

What can I do?

But the mouth of the blue dog is bound beforehand. How can I know this "beforehand," and serve its purposes so no one will be bitten?

What should I do?

"Bringing along with me where I have been" is the name of a river, not a man.

They sit and smoke cigarettes at a table. They are tired. This is the same as a tree. No dog. They go upstairs and sleep. No dog.

But this love goes out. A center is not to be protected, a center is not a goal. A center radiates.

He looked at the white face she'd shown him and knew: I have never seen this face.

Love?

A kind commitment to how things are.

HALLOWEEN: THAYER STREET

Those things that come from the other world
are here now. It is Halloween and turning midnight
where Lovecraft moved, clocking their arrivals
into the Age of Monsters, this century of pain.
They walk by in their Star Wars masks
their beast noses their bare legs their sexy
loudness their bottles their determination.
Pleasure is so difficult. This is the work
from which the soul arises. I say it is good
to paint your face red and wear a springy tail
I say it is noise and this noise

conditions an arrival
from which the Old Ones can be inferred,
the flesh that lived before the Id, immigrants
from eternity who sprawl here still
with tentacles to feel us up
that are exactly our veins our nerve cells strung
through the dark Christmas of our meat. Moon
over what has never yet been crazy enough.
Our sanity lures them. They extend themselves

through our limbs to encounter one another,
night neighbors, us. There is no difference.
It is sad for me, a little wistful
that the monsters do not come,
that they are here already, always.
I wanted them to be physical, out there, arriving
still sick with their hopeless geometries,
alien, appalling, true. I am tired
of worrying these spaces. I am tired
of being frightened of just us.

A STONE WALL IN PROVIDENCE

for Mary Caponegro

1

At dawn the sun investigates the blue copper dome
of the Christian Science church and at nightfall

the same formal acorn inhibits the roseate light.
Then it is dark. It is winter. The long propositions

of romance, as much a part of us as cracks in glaze
are part of porcelain, become hard to see in this light.

Hard to hear. The heart is always an investigation.
Let me draw inferences from difficulty. What is hard

is always beginning and comes to an end no more
than the pattern on the scarlet Bokhara carpet does

though it meets its ornamental border and resumes
all the alternative directions its mystery is heir to

thing after thing. So that is what it is: a city new
with fresh air, streets starting to be familiar,

shapes of people always familiar but the air of them, the style
tells me I am in this place, a hope of its own,

grace of its own. Isolate in openness, in the hope of change,
old me in a new city, selfish as colors.

2

A town where streets live up to their names is heavy
like reading a book that takes itself seriously, aesthetics,

grammar, politics. In this town I'm quizzical about my own
name, destiny, reputation. I am a part . . . yes, of that power

that stands to kiss the good and shapes the will instead.
Under the porcelain crucifix the light is keen, candlestick,

milk glass, the imputation of innocence because our eyes
do not analyze the surface deep enough. There is always more

and to such amplitude the simplisms of morality do not reach.
Dare not. What is done in the Mass! How dare the man the wine

the bread the haughty differences make identical! How dare we
be so confused? To bring to one bed so many women as if

never even changing the bright sheets or if they washed
                                                                themselves
a city! That is how it is, the integrals of danger. I love you

becomes a manifesto, even a theology. Be multiplicitous and
                                                                prophesy:
the world is one we know so many of by virtue of this quivering I.

                    3

About that power: it is the serum of questioning
that flows through the blood of the mind. The mind is current

through all flesh, it is a river, it is this river,
slaty pewter, sluggish under the arches at Fox Point

slowly getting around to be sea. The mind is its occasions,
faithful to the cloth and to the swell of hip

that minds the cloth. It is not nowhere. Cleverness of water
to pry everywhere is also its cunning. It can freeze a season

but there is always spring. The dome comes back at morning
far beyond the huge playing field where the girls at hockey

trot with cold red knees under plaid skirts with civil squeals.
And the mind has something to work with again, weary

of the ulcerating languages of night it gnaws at, strange grammar
whereby three a.m. turns into sleep and sleep into dawn

like one long sentence in whateverese.

4

Like so many codes it is mediated by a wall, an arduous
separation between the world and the world. There they play

and in its hither shade a pair of lovers lies down (or one
lies down and one kneels over) on this suddenly hot day

and beyond them and unseen by them in their slow parade
(he presses her belly lightly with one hand) the field

is full of summery english grass, hurdles, goals, foul lines
and no people. He stands now, she lies, the shadow

would be too cold for me but I am made of it, complected
of its sinister night body here in the high autumn afternoon.

I think they have lain down in me. Whatever they think of
is what I must say—I dont have to say *I* any more, every item

and every relation cannot fail to speak my dialect of mind.
And they go through their own morphologies, lovers, friends,

bodies making comfort for each other in what privacy they find.
They do what lovers do. For instance they are gone.

5

There is a wall we walk along to come home. Finding way.
The thing you see, the yellowing young oak, promises to be there,

promises a presentness, indexes a past a whole myth of causation
—acorn—gardener—weather—nurture—light, and as wind fusses it

argues a future in which it will govern a whole range of meanings.
For instance: that tree, do you remember that, by the old wall,

the way it looked, when the field suddenly filled with baseball
and the tree did not change, symbol of great Jupiter, the power

of being about what is on your mind unswervingly. This tree
is my authority. What we need to answer is what asks.

What I need to marry is what comes along. A thing is time.
A thing is a momentary rest between unending contradictions

that intersect in it, cross over each upon other, and regress
into the two directions of our fancy. Thing stays. Times goes,
comes.

6

A body when it sleeps becomes a stone, and when she reads
a book she is invisible. This discipline of bodies and of light,

the oldest science. What the cave mouth saw. And what the dog
was lured from wildness to worship, the way people move,

the way they seem to have something on their minds as they
move
with quick supple pacing from end to end of the enclosure

against the smouldering light. Where is she when she reads?
What does the dog think then, waiting some sign to recognize?

The astral body has been traveling, comes back slowly
to the waking body of one who has been napping, last light, who
wakes

to see the mackereling southwestern sky and one who wakes
                                                    beside him
says a horse a horse you can hear it clopping by. Dark shape

in the street, unmistakeable. Dark sound. A rider but not seen.
Who rides this horse? Where has the astral body been that now

so reluctantly returns to take control of this soft mineral,
this waking person who is nothing at all yet but the horse he
                                                    hears?

            7

Then what is this stone? How does it think? Or when they are
                                                    together
is that thinking, what they do in each other, where he pressed
                                                    her

as she lay lax under the wall and he knelt above her, two friends
in the conspiracy of shadow? Is that what is called thinking?

Suppose there really is an astral, a body like a pair of arms
leaping for the sky, out of the body like a story out of a book

when the book falls closed and the woman who's been reading it
is full of the adventure and her mind belongs to that place, those

voices. Suppose that body travels and we call its voyage "dream"
and then comes back to us minutes after waking and fills the
                                                    slow flesh

with a sense of itself and what it wants. It is almost painful
to have that visitor come back. Pins and needles. Always
                                                    something

new out of Africa. Rubadubdub of the new desires squeezing
into the convenient old places of the sleepstonewall. Did you say
                                                    horse?

Are you my lover? There was thinking but it went to sleep. Then
there was sleeping and it woke. There was still a sky. A city

lifting its outline into it dome by steeple by modern tower
still as a woman reading a book. Full of a story it woke to lose.

8

And when it's not a wall it is a way
because it's important not to be easy. To steal things from the
                                                              light!

And call that morning. The sky is textured here
so much given in old cities — *I am older than any* — who speaks?

Has a right to jettison its yesterdays but keep intact
the arrived-at texture of today, that lucid compromise

the best we have. A wall is reflection. A wall
is the son of a proud mother and he is proud.

By him they find a parking space in dream,
climb Mont Cenis, hear the clear voice of Judas lecturing

in the arctic athenaeum. We are always old and I am always
                                                           young.
Under the consenting oaks they come to parley

intelligence on intelligence. Man on man. Know the sex of walls
and know the organ of human policy: where the wall goes.

What the wall says. For distinction delights in self-proclaiming.
It is not that intellection is a ravening wolf. It is a dog

full of provisional chumminess. It is a dampness in this morning
                                                               air.
To think lays on the cherrywood drum table by the window a
                                                          fine dust.

9

It is a desperate act to be among my kind, cafe.
Two back to back working, a third squeezes between — women,
                                                        wisdoms.

For wisdom is by no means single. There is no ultimate
                                                        agreement
except to keep talking. Keep the fasts of time, the purple ferias
                                        that make me strange

wondering who died in the night. Who came to life?
What moves the light to break like news

upon us in the shapes of them hurrying through a pattern
that can be decoded, long after, memory tracking the bee paths

how the three women move behind the counter, leaving traces
                                                        that recur,
themselves as formal interruptions of this formless thinking.

Or behind veiled windows still translucent families move
through the warfare of their interactive distances, psyched-out
                                                        gazeteer

of chance apartments channeling their anger and granting such
                                                        peace
as space has in its mercy to bestow: bringing close, leaving far, a
                                                        soft corner

to feel sorry for myself in, sick, or lick the wounds. And in the
                                                        mean
called time among all this yummy flurry I like so well, the wall
                                                        stands.

10

Its evident stillness we are told is pure deception, a covenant of
                                                        molecules
to align in such a way that we are tricked by a shimmer of
                                                        solidity

and hence keep off the grass. Do not see (except from here, high
window)
the centerfielder suddenly appear to catch a fly then vanish back
of trees

from which their languid cries lift softly (storm windows already
down)
to curse the undercurrent silence. That was Pindar's golden harp,

a shout of the exerted body suddenly plucked from the silent
bowl of sky,
a noise out of which narrative uncoils. Decode this music. Say
what the shout

means to say, your father's black-sailed ship, your romance with
that sly Cappadocian hero. How your mother watched a snake
unfold

down near the waterfall and from its springtime stretch decided
she would make you with your father's instrument. Every noise
notates.

What we hear is seldom what is there. It is an index of some
history
we strive to know, and by knowing unite it with our own future
till

time and memory are one thick strand united, stubborn as a wall,
and just this endless self-referring rope or running it is my will
to break.

11

We come back at last to the simplest knowing:
a window pretending to be a self in a world of selves.

The things that hurt us are easy to remember,
a foot, a tooth, a number. A dentist in Paris

who did not listen to your pain. A need. I have lain
beside you and not known. We have not known

and all the same the field across Arlington
fills up with light, a marching band, a forest of rooftops

to say some last farewell to an immense city
we will go on living in, live forever, in, though

at this moment and in this eye it goes from us
passing in slate grey and umber and blue.

Shade comes through the window too, for all the hot porches,
yellow walls, graduate students at deft affairs next door.

Do not forget me, treetop, though you fall your leaves
and drown the book of my attention beneath the waves of light.

                    12

But are they waves, and so on. Is it a self, and so on.
Was it Lucerne where you became a woman, with all the hot
                                                        habit

of the lap, the business of bleeding? Was it Lausanne?
The things I talk about are seldom true, but the talk is true.

There is no fixed self in the stream of happenings—
does light happen to the crystal or does the crystal

happen to light, this multiform manyface hangs in your window,
pear-pointed, rotund, swaying, but not enough to break the calm

of white into the messages of color. No fixed self
but one can be made, is that it? That a rock can sit in a stream

and for all its moss and weathering be different from what
                                                    weathers it,
is that the destination of such histories as

it was Lausanne, you became a woman while the soft Swiss
mouths
inhabited their other language and you had no one to tell.

Who happened to you? Was what would become me already there
as mountain or sputtering rented car or over-attentive waiter

waiting for the woman you are? Maybe the talk is true,
truer than the nervous silence that sleeps me streaming.

13

It is seriously another place, seriously minded
to discover the least deflection of what this sun so seriously

takes to be real. I agree with its every syllable, every color
is accurate to the original design, unfailingly. The crystal

tells me so. Listen to the lattice. Listen to numbers
which are the reddest of our concepts, bloody number

by our Lady blessed. Pure threeness seizes the mind
and by what you feel then you know where the mind is

and what it does. It is seized, the virgin victim of experience,
hotel of what happens. I think of the thick white glue

that dries transparent, we look at what it joins
and forget they have been joined, that they are compounded

of a thick white spurt and its power to associate.
A toddler and its father (elder brother) walk by the hockey goal

Two black dogs frolic in the hockey field. Heaven is what
happens.

14

Since all trees look dead in the winter you cant tell till spring
which one will wake and which one will stand a while

all too cogently commenting on the season by being
that some-other-time we identify below the word "death."

15

I will tell a different story about space.
I will not ask the wall to tell my truth.

I will stand what it can tell me stone by stone—
that it is here to give me pleasure

as those lovers last time knelt and stood and lay and crouched
beneath its shade on that one warm October day—

were they making love or were they pretending
(I wonder sometimes how much pretending all love is,

the things we say or try to keep to ourselves
quiet as the skin rustling against skin)

basking in this pleasure of a wall. Why wall?
A wall to hold the banked-up earth in

where joggers run by now in squadrons
inside their sweatshirts young, official

athletes of an institution that learned Greek through Germany
a hundred years ago and got the curious idea

that it was the body that remembered, that if you train
the body to be true, healthy, full of grace

then somehow the paradigms of Sanskrit verbs,
the mysterious distinctions of a Plato, become its nature

and as it flexes its limbs in this fine sunlight
you can recover from the skill of it all ancient rightness.

16

Wall, stone, house, room, window, sun: how
could any of that be wrong? They run and that's right.

Blue sky, contrail, soft stratus in the west,
where could mistake be, old flaw? The only dicey thing

is what I say about it—there's the risk: to speak at all
and to inherit from such talk all sorts of edges,

odd discriminations, needless judgments, sins,
until I get so confused with me and thee and wall

that I cant call the color of the grass
the oxydizing copper of the dome or name

this girl who runs past now, outside, in mufti, all
those runners in their arcane spurting. What I know is staying.

17

Philosophy is such a place, the mind is such a place
that does not have its corners clearly marked

but it has its corners, its doors, its dust
from antique stucco work that sifts down year by year

almost invisibly, the crumbling that things do.
But we do not, or not exactly. We are strong, we last,

we change, we stay the same, grow rough, turn smooth,
capable of everything and sometimes impotent,

thin, fat, rejoicing and failing, we accomplish
and fall flat, all things conceivable and nothing done,

we sleep all the time, have insomnia, snore through the alarm,
wake up at midnight with dry throats jabbering,

too much, too little, diet, drunk, disordered, lascivious and
                                                        chaste,
prone to rapture, hold close, hold loose, hang tight and fall.

Nothing is true of us because these words are so—
we are as definitionless as god.

We struggle, sometimes, and sometimes we let go
and where we go when that great let is gone

is only where we were forever, where we are, beginningless,
always here, where the window lights up the wall.

18

A wall is something like pure staying. Pure distinction
that separates only what we mean to have divided

by the ground rules of our game. You are no ontology, you wall,
you are no distinction such that we could not, right now,

unpiece you stone by stone, until we see light just
past your shoulders, light that has no knowledge of a wall.

I think right now a wall is pleasure
is meant to give us some the way it gave those lovers shade

and in the shadow of our pleasure, given, shared,
the world of things takes on dimension.

I think things come from us, I think the joy we take in them
gives objects thickness, depth, height, color, texture.

Without us I think they're just ideas,
boring categories of somebody's momentary guesswork.

120

Think of the pleasure of a stone, our bodies touching.
Infer from that the pleasure of a wall. Infer a room.

19

How late is it? A black boy runs across the field.
Winterness. The southwest dome is flat, a green upwelling

like an Indian idea, a temple roof in Lucknow, green
great Stupa flatness, breast with a small gold nipple, cupola.

What is singing now? How late the mind has grown
with all its instances. Here I am. The unresolvable

contradictions of being anywhere. Here and not there.
This language and not that. Unprofitable distinctions kept

by the grammars of dying languages. Case endings of the moon.
He runs. It is a world of sheer vestiges. Sundays. What is gone.

20

So under the anemones a woman is studying her book.
Under its roof a house sits dreaming of slate. The rock dreams
                                                        moss.

Now I know you, wall. You are the sentence spoken in
                                                childhood,
ground onto the blackboard with wartime chalk, the verdict,

sentence of forgotten words but whose shape teaches every
                                                proposition.
What better sense could I make? Proportion. Architrave, dusty

giant bodies of the gods. Or is all the body dusty, chalk dusty,
and all the books, their gutters full of the dust we use to think?

When a god knows his death is near, dust falls on his brocade.
His armpits give off suddenly the smell

of all the sweat the workman he never was poured out
in honest but unmindful labor. His guitar strings come untuned.

And therefore I look at this squat dome and say again
how precious this sort of life is wherein it can be said:

A black boy runs and I am he. A dog runs with him and it is me.
I see him and am seen and am the seeing. In which the method
comes:

To cherish every difference and know there is no difference.

Providence,
3 October–22 November 1981

122

Saying
is elegy

when I hear
my own voice
on the tape
speaking
the words
that through me
fell
upon the page
I hear a sad voice

I dont feel sad
no sadness I know
no muscle of dense
conflict wedged
like beeswax
in a warm rock
dripping
these sad words down

not from my heart
the sorrow
falls
but from is it
the heart of the world
that she so speaks of
Mary

is the world's heart sad
or is it in us
as it is in mirrors:
when my right hand lifts
it is the left
that answers

so is all this sorrow I hear
liquid in my voice
just the mirror image of the joy
the world's heart is?

Let it be bliss.
Let it be this.

LOOKING

Once when I read the funnies
I took my little magnifying glass
and looked too close.

Forms became colors and colors
were just arrays of dots
and between the dots I saw the rough bleak
storyless legend of the pulp paper
empty as the winter moon

and dreaded it.
I had looked right through,
when I wanted a universe
that sustains
looker and looking and the seen
forever, detail after detail
never ending. And all I had found
was between. But between
had its own song:
Find it in the space between—

it is just as empty as it seems
but this blankness is your mother.

To my friends when I am eighty-five

and my night comes, please
dont harden your hearts against me
in the vice of politeness.

Lead me into the trees instead and say
Robert, we will walk in these nice woods.

Then leave me there with weasels and the moon.

ENEMIES

for Julie Coughlin

It is amazing. Life is as full of enemies as a tree with birds in springtime. These enemies wake us with quick noises but are gone by the time our eyes are open. We look around the empty room with bleak puffy morning eyes. There is a bird outside singing, but you cant count on it.

Then we get up and shuffle towards the bathroom. The enemies have left dust on the bare boards and our naked feet feel the soft difference. The enemies have chilled the tile of the bathroom floor then, and that wakes us a little further. Inside the sink pipe, the enemies sing loud, a whining then a triumphal snort, the whinnying elephant of water gushes too cold onto our warm hands. The enemies have in-stalled a mirror above the sink, and this tells its own lugubrious story. *There I am again*, we say, and see reflected behind us the soft morn-ing moving window light of our enemies, filtering through the cur-tains into the room

On the cream cheese the enemies have deposited a few crumbs of bread from a recent meal. One of these gets on our toast and releases a tiny microcosmic taste of sesame when a seed is crunched. One thin hair from an enemy is coiled over the fingerhole of the coffee mug, necessary to unwind it and discard it. The enemies throw a sheen of light on the surface of the coffee when we finally get it to our lips, the plip plip of the filter still noising on the stove. We drink.

Then a friend comes and leans on the doorbell a long time and we know that once again we have been saved from our enemies.

1

The upper octave of the long cross-flute
is feminine. On it you hear played
"Gesar moves northward." An old
song haunts the breath the way
the words we say and say recur, and air
mutters around these fallen rocks.
The lower register they say is male
and hard to play.

2

For once the night is mine.
The tower I reared once
I opened to the wind, wind
brought birds and birds brought song
of theirs to silence me a while.

It is good, love, to listen to,
they sang, and good to argue
with your ears.

            "The Stone Companion,"
"The Rain of Stairs," "What
this Vulture Heard above the Peak,"
"Men Fly on Feet," "The Flower
Beneath Me Like the Mouth of Hell,"
"From their Tables I Snatched the Sense
of Word and Left their Empty Bread."

3

I answer by going to the wall
that old magnificence who sings.

"And when they wake, the monks
play the instrument they like best"
until it is day
and the flute is subsumed in light.

                4

The notes I took were lost, some in the snow, some in the quick young
river when the Christmas thaw dissolved the snow. A few I still have,
bits of paper and marked cloth I had about my person or written in
safer ink. I transcribe them here line by line. There is much I forgot,
but nothing here I dont remember.

                5

Flowers brought to the lama have a way of lasting longer. Perhaps,
a modest man, he doesnt wear them out with looking.

                6

I trust the radical
explanation

birds in the trees.

Needing quiet, the men of old
invented flowers, those exquisite
sugars, made bees to tend them
& subsume our little noises in their hum

On this they rode or strolled
till language with its soft permissions
ripened in their mouths—

words come
when the mouth hears

and language stills the mind
the way the bees attune
the myriad remarks of all the flowers
into one clear slow nourishment

*

die into speech
as the greenworld
dies into winter
any color just
a taste in the mouth

honey on a spoon

*

I study
by writing

down

between
the last light
and the first

an autumn sky

*

the word hidden between syllables
crane on a misted-over lake

a crystal chained
to being seen
sways in the wind of nobody looking

*

this play of sound
bird's work
cracking the enamel of the lake

*

duck for it
find it between
what I say & what I mean

ORPHÉE

I have a right to lust for anybody I like. I have a right to lust for you.
You hold this in your beige fingers while your other hand nimbles
the keif to your soft lips. Beyond this page your thighs stretch towards
the window, skin packed with the squirm my lust is interested in.
All the light comes from the window. I have a right. You're reading
against the light, my words are rhythmic obscurations of the pure
light. Didnt your mother tell you not to read against the light? You
should be spanked. I tear off the panties you've been wearing since
yesterday, the mint-green ones with the fabric separating from the
elastic over the right hip. But at the sight of your intelligent ass pois-
ed for the blow, I relent. I have a right to relent, to perceive you
through the glamorous dreamworld of your underwear. Stop blow-
ing that fume at me, you know I dont smoke that stuff, it's hard
enough for me to be coherent as it is. But since your clothes are off
now and there's plenty of light from the window reflecting off your
belly, let me read you a poem I wrote while you were asleep. I have
a right to write. Listen:

> The room is hot enough
> for just a sheet
> to shape itself to you
>
> what does it feel like
> to be in your body
> especially when you're sleeping
>
> you snore a little
> like a phone
> ringing in the house next door
>
> on a summer night
> soft before puberty
>
> I wonder
> if I will ever answer you

You have a right to be awake now and doing what you want. I have a right to lust for someone and then for silence. To read what no one writes—that is to be at home in the world. I have a right. The world is an old letter from a friend you find unexpectedly under your nose. You read it, you have a right to read it. Later you remember you wrote it yourself.

GETTING THERE

for Susan Quasha

1

Look for me when the birds see me coming
I will be the first one you see come out of dream

holding a glazed green bowl you gave me
to store the rice of my conceit in
& bide the long water

      where is boiling?
   where is rice?
       plain rice, the kind the Chinese
in their whimsy polish
knowing something better than good for you

a luminous white sacrifice
accepting the stain we know as taste?
        where is food
      the sustaining actor
   who guides our play
into the industrial revolution of the body
         to bide the outcome
beige people in blue air,
America?

2

It is always the worst time to be born.
I know, I was there,
I sweltered through the womb and public school,
there was no end of conversation, I lost
my puberty in museums, my virginity
was a public library of renewable delinquency,
my manhood was fire in an oildrum

134

while the snow blackened Bleecker Street.
Working night and day for twenty years
I became a shelf of books that pays alimony.

            3

So I assure you I know how it is. We are together
in the worst of times, this paradise
of intricate perceptions, this accountancy of ecstasy
we undertake to be masters of
writing everything down, perfect ledgers, not a nub
of moss out of place, rocks in our Japanese garden.

I sympathize. I too have birthdays.
I too am a mink coat looking for the Primordial Mink
to give my glory back to. I too am hair.

            4

I think I am trying to seduce you
to stay in this tiresome bed.
What would they do without us,
our thinly disguised omniscience,
our powerful afternoon naps
that dream them into place.

                    I project on you
in dubious sisterhood.
                    So that's why I didnt get to your party,
busy dreaming up excuses
                    and why not?
Since the whole kosmos is a network of symbolic behaviors,
lila, let me
            have round me
    those who are symbolic as fruitcake,
full of excuses and explanations and sweet lies,
            their soft wet mouths
        full of the silence called language.

History is something to take shelter in
from the sun of immediate confusion
and find the bliss of form—
a book so thewed
that the caressive medicine
which is the cool shade of any tree
in any given summer
does not loose its limbs.
He had been writing it all his life
first red then black then red again
the banners of all his women all his ever
women from the earliest when had it begun
and then a final act of red indebtedness
that said Everything I am
is simply a consequence of you.

What could words mean (these words)
if they meant that?
                    Is there no end
to hurrying up avenues, drunk after dinner,
in cold wind at any season, to be there
in the lobby of her quarters
awaiting the same shuddering elevator
to a floor high enough above civilization
to show a block away one dark roof
where someone moved, who?

"Why dont you come to me before dinner?
Why does there have to be beef on your breath,
I dont mind the wine?"

                    He turns from the window,
his elbow veronica'd in a billowy white curtain
and says nothing. If you knew
what I know you'd be silent too.
She understands that. She too
has lived all her life in the city.
It is there. It is simply there.

TWENTY

for Jessica Bayer

How could I have known and what is there to know
worth separating men (in kitchen) from women (on porch)
at a party such that while all of them are still quite young
each feels about all the others terribly "They are old"

knowledge of people is the hardest meanest cunning
and thank god most of us can slip it off like a shirt or a skirt
just being naked of all our experiences and sort of open
to what will happen as meager as we guess it will be

it will just be more knowledge more experience to shuck off
sometimes after a party you throw out the guests' unfinished
                                          drinks
before the ice cubes are even melted though they've lost their
                                         edge
and they hit the lawn softly and wetly you go to bed almost
                                         dawn

or else if you're drunk or want to be you finish all the glasses
yourself and ask "Who am I anyhow?" and just to ask
the question is satisfying as if someone had told you his name
and you had no reason for disbelief except he looked so sincere

why are we trying to trick each other we care we care
even for each other why is the porch light still on
the bed should be chill and austere it isnt it's just a bed
to carry savage apartness across an average dark.

137

It was a cactus coming out of the ground, or more precisely a cactus growing out of another cactus, from the smaller a pale red flower budding, full of yellow-pink filaments.

That was the story. He had to invent a woman to tell it, a room for her to take her clothes off as she told it. A room full of smoky light, the woman's rhythmic movements, half conscious, half athletic, culminating in her naked, sitting on the edge of the bed, swinging one leg up, under the sheets as the flower opened.

Is this enough? Should there be someone there to hear it? "Arent the words of it enough? Let the words listen. It will do them some good to hear themselves spoken."

But how could the same old words bear to hear again the same old images? Only the breath was new. It was for instance raining out, raining hard as the year fell into February. And this very rain, cold as it was, freezing at once on the slick dangerous roads, was still a sign of spring, a great relenting. And that is the oldest story of all. Why should these poor cactuses and this woman worry or be abashed when a year itself is all about flowering?

So it seemed. But in hearing a story one wants to think that somewhere there is another story not being told—not just hiding behind the told story or inferable from it, but a wholly different story, intact, unimaginable, flesh.

The effect of heat on smoke. Cigarette smoke circling up into the shade-cone of the tensor lamp is violently disturbed, billows down He thinks each time it's a moth or a sluggish winter fly. Story of fly in winter. Story of a house's old white wood.

FIVE PRECIOUS STONES

From the blue air an emerald condenses. In it I see, facet by facet, my father stirring oatmeal by the kitchen stove, shaking dry nutmeg on it from a tin box. I do not see him eating. Outside the window, shaggy with ivy, the last roses of a Brooklyn autumn catch in yellow the early light. When I see this I know that half my heart is healed.

From the red air a ruby is focused held in the palm of a white hand. I see my bride winding her mauve sari about hips and shoulders. This ruby sends a ray to meet me. Now the time is soon to take a bride, but soon is a sea with many waves. These images I've stored in mind are brideprice. Am I willing?

> Equal air for equal extract.
> Tincture of cloves,
> golden seal.
> An orange peel.

Do I silence other people's work in them? Why am I not collaborating? Why do I work so hard alone?

> Hard as a maple tree in January
> silently lifting
> for its own sake high
> a juice that feeds you.

The green air condenses a sapphire in which I see myself able to do. Open a letter from a friend and read: "You can do this, do me, my mind lies open to you as my body. It is the same as understanding." In another facet of the stone I see this river at twilight in August, bay at my feet thronged with water-caltrops. A water-lily spreads its petals as I watch, a pale blue skyey color not wet by what it rests above. I see a friend weeping, her tears discrete as crystals on her cheeks. "This grief," she says, "is not a question. Do not solve my feelings. See."

Then from the yellow air a padparadschah appears, orange corundum, rarest of stones. No one is like me, I realize. And no one is like anyone. We are equivalent in our awesome difference. Be kind to me, causality.

139

A bunch of leaves
caught in the storm window
winter birds.

Then there is air, empty, lucid. All resemblances dissolve. Who would facet nothingness? The diamond tells. All its light is ray, the rays read me, reach here. The source light of emptiness illumines somethingness here. All I am is what it sees.

SCION

The son says:

"Vote for my father. If he can forgive me, he can do anything." They hear him and are impressed.

Slush lines the tall sidewalk protected by a railing. Post office, the hardware. They look at the thermometer.

"He is a good man, and I am a good boy now. I have a smooth stone in my pocket—can you guess what kind, what color?"

They try to guess. They are wrong.

"It is carnelian but red, like blood. I have a new sweater, see?"

They study the sweater, blue and red, a herd of white reindeer stiffly crossing his chest.

"My mother brought it home from Norway. Did you know I was part Norwegian?"

They study his face, looking for fjords, hard bones, midnight sun.

"I love my reindeer." He strokes his rib cage, the deer rumple and smoothe under his fingers, still heading west.

"You all know my father's father's father built the mill in this town. I guess you know about my grandmother."

She had gone away, no one knew where, and came back wealthy. There were two fortunes then in town, both in the same family.

"She started the Eastern Star lodge. It used to be over the liquor store. It stopped in the war, they stopped meeting. That was when I was born, the war."

They knew this. They remembered the war. The machine gun in front of the Legion post, painted aluminum, clean-looking even in snow, reminded them.

"But nobody seems to know how this town got its name."

They were no wiser.

If she went down to the town
& came back in green
her mother'd brush her red hair
saying "There, there, no one

is busier than you, no one paler.
It all is a farm, my daughter."
Then the cows would take over
lowing & moving their feet

vague on the messy concrete.
"Milk me" they'd think
"in our turn, we churn
constantly the sky inside us."

And daughter would hear
& wonder why here was so far
from there, the town from the farm,
the hand from the hand.

"We are distance only, mother.
Everything else is green.
I have to go down again
to catch my lover's eye again."

"And who is he this time?"
the mother said. "Oh he is changed,
mother, you'd never know him,
he is not the man you knew.

He is dark who had been fair,
his hair is long now & he wears
a twisted ring you gave him once.
He eats his food with cinnamon,

seldom seldom does he talk to me.
I will go down to him again
but there's no hurry. Tell me
all over what you know

before I go, tell me winter
& what cows are really for,
& food & bodies. Tell me
with your hands in my hair."

A mark on paper
lasts as long as the paper

a mark on air
lasts a long year

these birds are erasing the sky

THEN

If a flower could walk
independent of a lover's hand
or an army of bouquets
invade the red land, straggling
up the foothills to the border

or if the animals we see
so deeply rooted in the moment we see them
were in fact grown there only there
to be on hand when we open our eyes
a horse a sheep a dog full of perhaps

or if the stone we sit on the first
day of thaw had called us to itself
and we were just the pronouns in
its long sentence, and we hear it

and gloss it as the pasture, morality,
the dialectic, or if the picture in a book
were a quick eye examining us
before it winks its pages and goes on

or if the phone that never stops ringing
were an ear itself just checking our silence
like mother pausing at night by the nursery door
or if the piece of bread I eat were a brave

explorer leaving the familiar airy light
for a research expedition into the ordinary dark
they hear about with dread, yet dare to enter
and go and go and never come to the end

THE ANGEL OF THE DIALECTIC

for Laurie Durante

I told a friend: Poetry, like love, is the triumph of imagination over experience. The lover must maintain the double Vision: the secular girl in time, Beatrice in eternity. Similarly, poetry must observe the secular fact (common language) and the Splendor (grammarye or magic) that shines through it—both are true. Or more precisely, only both together are true. If the lover (or the poem) chooses only one, he (or it) succumbs to logic without warmth; if to the other, to obfuscation and impenetrably personal symbolisms of projection: rhetoric. The angel who mediates, unifies, and thus presides over the bothness of love, of poetry, is the Angel of the Dialectic.

She answered: I am convinced. Daphne, to flee masculine logic (Apollo) gave herself up to the remorseless organic feminine: the tree. Apollo mourns in his abstract aloneness, Daphne mourns in the never-ceasing rhetorical rustle of her leaves. But who is this Angel of the Dialectic? Did the Greeks know him?

I reached out and stroked her hip, and said: I am he, I am Dionysus. I caress but do not possess. I care but I do not claim. I am the ardent liquid of all life, fire of water, the juice of things, the processing. I am Desire that dissolves in dream, and common daylight that crystallizes to a diamond body. My wine is language, which touches every mouth and stays pure, itself renewed by the act of being used.

for Gina Maria Caruso

If dawn would only quiet me the host
of far having the little truth
tucked under the tongue the
peak experience train ride to Rouen

I saw her body stand up as a city
we were late for the assignation
or magic cauldron the deep word I dreamed
kelp strewn along the beach

of course she was a neck a truth
between clarity of mind and lust's
equivocations that so bruise the heart
of course how could I not caress

or your deep eyes the point of feeling
one glimmer constancy among the brave
architecture of so human face
of course the desperate planet

in shimmering light the gods we are
I have had to do everything myself the work
my own footstep Friday on the naked beach
and then being not so become full human

every man is an island but this sea
you sequin beds us in one uneasy sleep
because there is finally together there is
blue low smoke above the Norman plain

size of a platonic spool a twist of your
thread around my finger sometimes the hand
cancels the new intelligence of eyes
why did I want to touch so much

and make the creamy breakers rich with comings
I am American I live solely by the news
and gossip is my Genesis a mass of trifles
lifted to a drunken unseen god at morning

companion of wine-bibbers and harlots
a song and dance man of a somber sort
a gigolo of *Geist* this painting I enrol in
fierce colors of the other side of lust

I want your company in my lap of worship
we bring our own suspicions to the bed lovely
thieves for fear of being lonely contrive the wine
to share a tiny ecstasy and then be sober

what have you gotten started that I must end
and shape to share your body's moment
tender in late winter dialectic
"trees put on what we take off"

and then there are sermons in quiet houses
I do not understand a single word
this is another city investigations of a guitar
friendship's vacant arch unless you touch me

then is a far kingdom greenly close
and sheep walk like princes from their little brooks
and still are sheep are that strange color
a city grows when night makes free with it

I am allowing a meeting of our flesh the nerve
creates geography the navy of stray impressions
bombards my senses your skin so quick
flashes under memory's hemline a salty mouth

convenient to this telling this is the script
the image uses to contrive a house we live so fast
it would be silver with forgetting
remember me because there is no time at all

when there is touch there is no subject
there is nothing but the moon and sun
shining together in the western sky
until we have membership in red

it all comes home my dear does it not
the eloquent hips of our lost lovers the tender
eyes of friends who stayed the thick glasses
still smudgy from their paws an inch of stale wine drunk

measure by the falling light the means of falling
where what is sure convulses in a mouth sweet with saying yes
what species of releasement or dark falling
down through the spaces inside words.

EUCALYPTUS

Dont you remember? It was eucalyptus, but it wasnt Stockton. It was La Jolla, not warm but enough to take off clothes. It was a large grove of young trees on the edge of the campus, younger than the students even who idled by listening to cassettes and wondering how the surf is tonight. Warm enough among these blue-eyed trees. Your hair had been wet from the sea (and the sea wind was misty now, investigating our armpits) but was only damp now, resuming its supernormal fulness, the controlled wildness of its exuberant mass. If it wasn't you it was someone else. If it wasn't him it was me.

We snuggled on the sofa in your studio and I got fresh. Caressing me, you said there is another, but you didnt remember his name. We'll call him John. I said there are many others, I remember their names all too well but we'll call them you. It was clear we were making love no matter what the eucalyptus thought, or John a few floors above us compiling statistics on liberal attitudes towards El Salvador. You got up and locked the door and unlatched your skirt. Actually the other way round. I like it that you always wear skirts. I liked it that you took one off.

Let me taste your eucalyptus, I said, the well-hidden, the fragrant, the powerful, the young, the fresh. I know better words than those but I was flustered by the sight and sound of your skirt sliding over your hips on its way to the floor. Understanding my need, you said some of them for me. I have always admired your language. Your vocabulary is as rich as your hips. What could you do with my big furry head in your lap? You rested your fingers in my hair and liked me. You said some words: squall; relent; inveterate; lambent; pirouette; sequester; larrakins; shivaree; callipyge; turmeric; nettle; scramasax; slowly; seizure; orphrey; talmud; toluene; kittiwake; kestrel; initiate; gallinule; awn; polyglot; furrow; aumbrey; tabernacle; cusp; cenote; laudanum; spin. All the words I heard I used correctly in complete sentences and spoke them into you, along with some words of my own. Look in your lap and you'll remember.

STANZAS

Upon whose accents do I marshall a small domestic beast
Someone who in fact is like a sailor but no water
Someone who is dry—Yak of the Kham plains or Dri its mate
Fierce Drong of the Takla Makan—
These names living wake me from the tomb
Consigned I was by dint of false connections
Those birds of false feather who flew me away
Ay ay they flew me away

One book after another it smelled of clean stiff bindings
WPA freeform inkform designs fresh after forty years unopened
Book is a word in which they sleep
Names wake me from the sleep of words
Another time round it was Queens and on foot
The sun on Liberty Avenue were there ever such shadows
Gaunt gothic of the el overhead sparks flew
Then the clean light of Elderts Lane the library close now
These names mean nothing to you

Stanza Two

So it is formal and faithful as a xerox something is lost
Some footstep I didnt find on Juan Fernandez a naked slim step
No one had been there before me there is no one there till I
come
We went to sleep holding each other tight
And speaking the names out loud of Russian cities
Including Ustyug Velikiy whose accent I'd always had wrong
Tell me a story that lifts from the dead
All names whose correct accents are seldom spoken
Durrell Nabokov Leskov Andrew Marvell whose avenue
Of white oaks continues to persevere
Through the serene madness of old forests right to my door

Door of my unlikeliest house the opposite of remembered
Nautical imagery through six hundred leagues of sleep

151

And then I am there in the garden of the soon-to-be-remembered
Whose names are feminine whose shadows are tweed and silver
Whose shadows are satin and nightfall and radish and now I
                                                    remember

    Stanza Three

It is not bad to be boring and to be dead
Has always this coming forth to commend it
This rousing to a new name soon to be spoken
You hear first in the squishy vagina of your mother
While your father is busy welcoming the dead
With his well-known grunts and beads of sweat in his mustache
Then you are born the book flops open again
My darlings consciousness never dies
It always goes somewhere else and this else is our business
Darlings our business is always this other
Reaching.

MOUNTED POLICEMEN

There are strange white people to be sure
There is a white space in my aromatic arm
Truth falls down that way between the hooves of the head
Smashing the tundra of that region treeless and white and serene
And a fordless river
Be adept of that white currency
I hear the ali kali while I sleep awakening is translation
Sometimes a whole day is a forgery
Sometimes a garbled redaction of a lost original
Sometimes the horses are white
They run as fast as they can no one runs faster
This is a space to be sleep in
A flower on fire that is the heart
Are you sure
Are you sure you can cross it without getting wet
Hung in the head is a lamp to be sure
Hung in the heart is a lamp to be sure
Are there four flames on one fire one fire on four flowers
Is it one is it white
This is what the horseman wonders patrolling the heart
Weeks by this forest no noise from inside

2

Precincts forest precincts sacred glade known by inference by
                                                             map
They must be up to something in there it's so quiet
What does the wonderer blank while he wonders
What monuments of sheer understanding crumble while he
                                                    busily thinks
This is the white country do I care where you are
Spurts among shadows shouts among thorns
They are coming he is certain what is his certainty worth
You are always far from where he is thinking
Because he sees your shadow slip over his mind
Something good to see shape of a taste in his mouth but quick

153

Quick in flurrying brush is it white is it white
Faltering down his old bone
He forgets the horse he sits on he forgets the tundra it
                                                    investigates
He wants to see the shadow while he's busy with the light

3

Sometimes the horse he's on is just one of the horses
A million horses every one of them white
And they are the forest patrolling itself
And he's just the sound in their heads of everything that is not
                                                          hooves
He is what is not running
He is white in their heads and they are his running
White inside white and all of them running
Sometimes white

4

He forgets where he rides
It is somewhere to be white
So that the white pours down inside him knowing the difference
All differences are surely white all differences are white
This is where he begins and the words fall
White after white down his newest throat
It is not worth while to be tired when you can be throat
Will you be my throat the white words coming into and out

5

Sunder something that is small and learn to be white with it
What white is comes down
Be white with what is coming down
Until the whiteness of it changes the music of your throat
You taste curry then and a black pine tree has nothing in it
Nothing of your white fear this is white just white

154

Just and white and white and fills you
He is filled with what is hungering to go down
So much comes down and only the white of it

6

I have never seen a policeman on a white horse
In my city white horses would certainly wear policemen
And policeman would wear a pink cape over his blue suit
He would be fine he would hold a golden whistle to his heart
At the sound of it all the white horses would come all the white
horses
Fill the streets of my city with white traffic

Those who are beautiful
A sonata
If even sounds have skin
A space some spaces give
Some who are beautiful because space

Sun's able to shape sequent light on wood mere
Ear squints to hear rightly rightly
Intonation of the sitting still
Some because space because wood
Glue gold hold what you said
My eye playing your lap
Space in your knee's time to hold
Sonorous what did you say?

A chaplet of amber noises
Humming around your neck
I would expect May in California
Heat I remember
Long roads northeast from the San Pablo
Into amazing rice

Something blossoms every month
Call it into my mouth
A little bleak a little bird
Taking self less serious
So I can take you
You look exactly like yourself
Equally white
Chaste nostrils in arc-en-ciel
It is better not to see than to obsess
Certain curves command my mind
And all time after repeats their sleek geometry
I grieve in those numbers except to hold
Better not to see than to possess
Undivided destinies we cant control
Fortune cookies on the plate distinguish text

This one for you that
One must be listening in the wood
Itself a sort of glass
Finger wet
Sings
A sort of forest
Under a sort of varnish all that color knows
A sort of company of potential friends or
So often it sounds as if it can't decide
Or as if deciding were not beautiful
Not half as beautiful as being

To be healthy is not necessarily to be
Or to be going or anywhere
To be healthy is only a woollen
Shirt in winter it is always winter out
Because some compression in the music
Faces glass
Her like exactly look you equal
Rainbow clothes better to see stretto
Fortune in the wood
The sound has sheen
The share is *schön*
You must be shimmering when you do that
You must remembering me when you hear that in your hands
Because our blues
Are very ravenous are you
Some bite and some drink the shape of the cup itself
Drink this drawing of you doing so

Rest a hair of color on a lot of air
Seed marigolds and wait for white
An obvious imposition on the mind
Keep me in your heart
To be this agriculture too
So many chitterlings in this cauldron
And my burnt thumb tastes you
Serene hysteric with large eyes
Immensely wise and hardly knowing
Now is the time

Before you get older or I get young
The way time's hydraulic flushes
Certainly leave large spaces
Or where would the music go
Lady blow me blue
The nature of what is personal imitates music
Fond father uncle of nine a desert
Advertises for its ruling rock
Come do my job I need some help
Sit up late taking me seriously
Every lover says obsess obsess
So I'll be no lover longer
And this quick kiss won't tie your hands

Any living room looks better for fish
There are slow release feeders for fish
We can leave the tank alone for days and not hurt fish
I swear Ladie my tongue is one of such
Fish and feeder both you'll find
Lambent in your fish bowl I your mica castle
And all I am is good for you again
Your house and never be possessed
Your hands and never be obsessed
Your nose and never be plain
Your hair and never be rage
Your arm and never be curt
Your belly and never be mute
Your knee and never be local
Your fingertip and never sand
Your two ears and never Solomon
Your important neck and never Tahiti
Do not hide your heart your navel and your left hip
Do not have a shy shank
Do not let your elbow learn Norwegian
Do not be wise o do not be wise
There are birds here that could make two of us
Dinner for a star and cheese for a child
Your eyelid and never a Ferrari
Your eyelash and never a boat
Your nostril and never philosophy

Your chin and not a postage stamp
Your tonguetip and never night
Shimmer o do not be wise
Grow young without apologies
Your buttock and never a bible
Your shoulderblade and no sheep
Your nape and no oracle
Never be wise o never
O shimmer and not relax
Be wise neither nor soft
Your ankle and never the Bastille
Your sex and never a senate
Your breast and never a prayer

All we have are the names of things
Not so
All we have are names and scarcely things
Scarcely things are for the having
Names are for the calling
Calling is beautiful and what we have
Is busy with calling

During the recent war there was some traffic in meat
During the opera what we had eaten began to sing
During history women changed their minds
There are so many alternate releases
There is time there is ink there is time
So some of some that are beautiful
Resist the resistance is beautiful
Things are remarkable things have come back
We are busy with calling
The resistance is ribbon blue-black for your hair
Scarlet grosgrain a stone at morning
A headache a bonsai these things are calling
Something red is calling a green book
Some sympathy is sure to be itself
O I am tired of not being loose
All these connections are freedom looselimbed mind
What is resistance resistance is a hedge
Resistance is sand under pine tree

Resistance is railroad
Matchhead a beach a guitar of a certain kind
Resistance is palm
Resistance is a cat howling in the cellar under a civil house
What is resistance
All these connections are freedom
A baby in a postcard tree
A passacaglia tied to the bed
Resistance is the shape of a ham upside down
What is resistance resistance is resin
It is often apricot it is masculine
Resistance is feminine is hawser is handkerchief
War is resistance what is resistance
Resistance is careful listening rarer than thought
Resistance is copper is numerical is number
What is resistance resistance
It is umber it matches it disguises it dispenses pills
It is ink
All these connections are freedom
Connection is freedom
That is equation not definition
Resistance is something to be equal to
A moment in sunshine like a seal on a rock
Resistance is something to go to the ocean with
Resistance complains to the waves
Resistance asks if it may speak
Resistance asks the sun to shine
May I shine says the sun may I shine says my voice
To the house if it listens
Resistance is trying to go
Resistance is gone
Ask the wood are you house and the music are you listening
If it is a house it listens
If it is music it hears.

Printed September 1983 in Santa Barbara & Ann Arbor
for the Black Sparrow Press by Graham Mackintosh
& Edwards Brothers Inc. Design by Barbara Martin.
This edition is published in paper wrappers; there
are 250 hardcover copies numbered & signed by the
author; 50 numbered copies have been handbound
in boards by Earle Gray, each containing a unique
holographic painting & poem by the author, from
the Fourth Series of *The Mirsuvian Calligraphies.*

Photo: P. Snyder

"Under words. I was wondering what lay beneath them, the things I said and meant and used, some of, only some of, to build poems. For years their surface had been enough, and then that history (half-fanciful, half-documented) we call etymology. But I wanted a spiritual etymology, to lead the word back—but not now to some Indo-European root, but to its root in my experience, mind in action, tree in the world. Words are narratives intact in themselves, and all the narrations and sequences here (more story-prone than before in my work) unpack the primal narrative each word tacitly persists in laying before me. This book's title is indebted to Starobinski's account of Saussure's long subtle studies of anagrams in Lucretius and Virgil, *Les Mots sous les Mots.* And to the excited turn in my life when I chose, for reasons only my poems talk about, to enter, 1980 and thereafter, my personal underworld, and report the word I heard there."

—RK

Robert Kelly was born in New York City in 1935. *Under Words* is his forty-fifth book. He teaches at Bard College in Upstate New York, and directs the writing program of the Avery Graduate School of the Arts.